By the same author:

George Thomas, Mr Speaker
The Memoirs of Viscount Tonypandy
(Century 1985)

MY WALES

GEORGE THOMAS
VISCOUNT TONYPANDY

PHOTOGRAPHS BY
SNOWDON

GUILD PUBLISHING LONDON

CONTENTS

ACKNOWLEDGEMENTS

I have been greatly helped in the writing of this book by all my friends in Wales, who spared their time and their memories. Due to my illness during the writing of this book, I relied heavily on the services of David Tytler to whom I express deep gratitude.

George Thomas

I would like to express my personal gratitude and thanks to my friend Mervyn Jones for his hospitality and all the time he so kindly spent taking me around South Wales, and for sharing his profound knowledge of the country; also to Martin Hill for his efficient and invaluable assistance while on location; Terry Lack for printing the black and white photographs so flawlessly; and in particular, Paul Bowden for his patience and care in helping choose and lay out photographs with his customary flair and talent.

Snowdon

FOREWORD

This book is not a tourist guide to lovely Wales – there are plenty of books about the sheer beauty of Wales. What I am trying to tell is the story of the Wales where I was nurtured and which I know and love. That place is a place of contradiction and challenge with its own sense of humour that is different from many other parts of the United Kingdom. It has its own characteristic spirit and compassion that has been fashioned out of crisis in generation after generation.

The small number of old photographs at the beginning show the Wales of my childhood, so very different from the modern landscape of factory estates, supermarket high streets and idle docks. They may surprise a younger generation unaccustomed to the idea of South Wales being the vigorous industrial area it then was.

Each generation in Wales seems to have had its own particular heartache. The miners in the Rhondda, the slate quarrymen in the north and, twenty years ago, the tragedy of Aberfan, a tragedy that wiped out a generation. On 21 October 1966, 116 children and 28 adults died. It was there, on the night of that terrible day, that I first met Lord Snowdon when he came unexpectedly to visit the bereaved families who were still in a state of shock. Some, even now, I believe still are.

We met again and worked together at the investiture of Prince Charles as Prince of Wales at Caernarfon Castle in 1969 where Lord Snowdon was Constable of the castle.

And now our friendship is renewed in *My Wales*. His photographs are not here simply to illustrate the words but to add his own perspective. Join us now on our journey through the Wales we know and love.

George Thomas
Cardiff 1986

North Wales

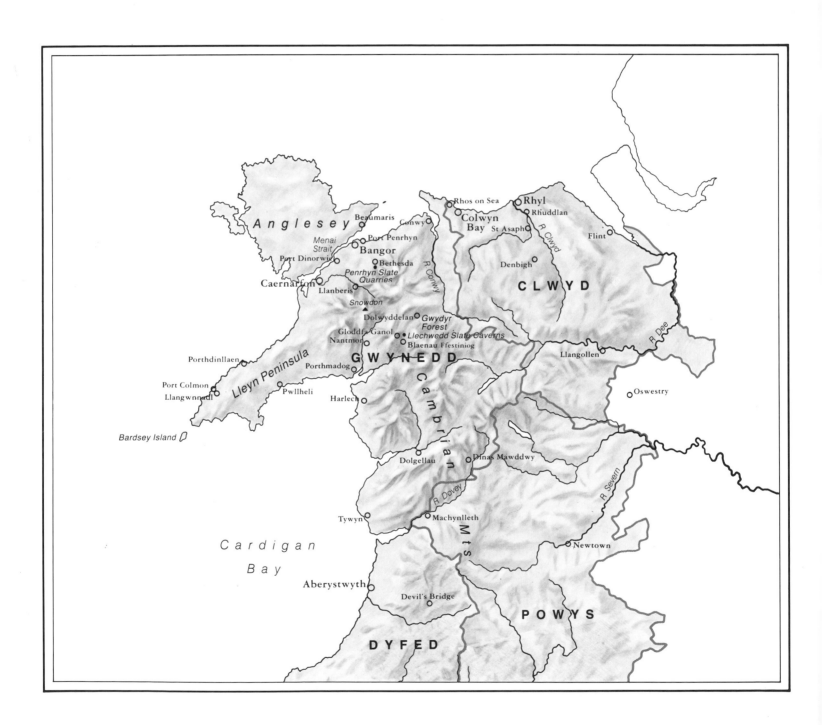

South Wales

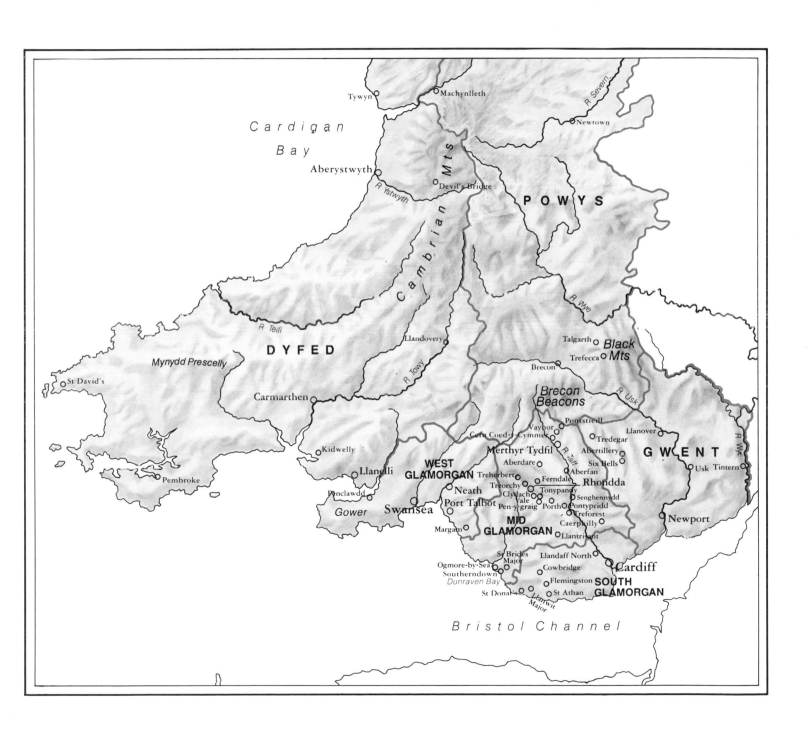

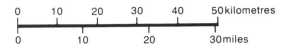

0   10   20   30   40   50 kilometres

0   10   20   30 miles

Cardigan Bay

Tywyn

Machynlleth

R Severn

Newtown

Aberystwyth

Cambrian Mts

Devil's Bridge

R Ystwyth

POWYS

R Teifi

Llandovery

Talgarth   *Black Mts*

DYFED

Trefecca

R Towy

Brecon

St David's

Mynydd Prescelly

R Wye

R Usk

Brecon Beacons

Carmarthen

Pontsticill

Vaynor   Llanover

Cefn Coed-y-Cymmer

Kidwelly

Tredegar

Merthyr Tydfil

Abertillery

GWENT

Aberdare   Six Bells

WEST GLAMORGAN

Llanelli

Treherbert   Ferndale   Aberfan

Usk   Tintern

Treorchy   Tonypandy   **Rhondda**

R Taff

R Wye

Penclawdd

Neath

Clydach   Vale

Senghenydd

Port Talbot   Pen-y-graig   Porth   Pontypridd

Gower   Swansea   Treforest

Margam   **MID GLAMORGAN**   Caerphilly   Newport

Llantrisant

St Brides   Llandaff North

Major

Ogmore-by-Sea   Cowbridge   **Cardiff**

Southerndown   Flemingston   **SOUTH**

Dunraven Bay   St Athan   **GLAMORGAN**

St Donat's   Llantwit Major

Bristol Channel

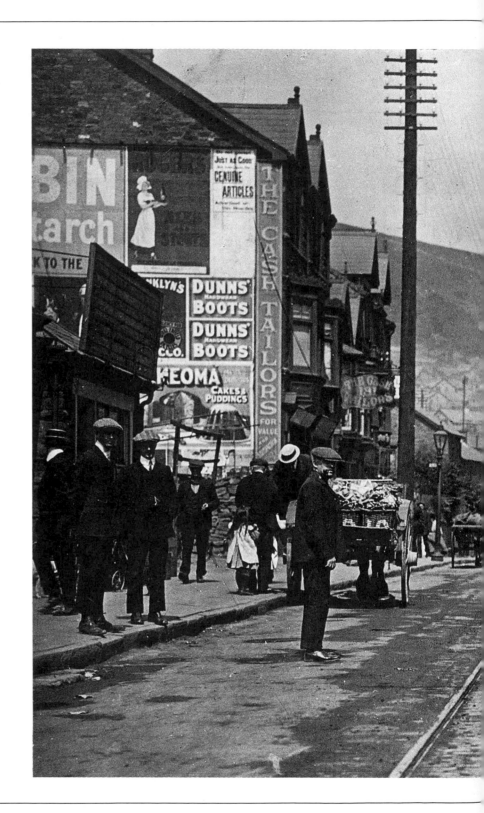

Main Street . . . the main road in Tonypandy, Dunraven Street, showing the tram lines. When I was eleven, we used to hold a penny raffle on a Saturday with a two shillings prize (10p) for the person who drew the number of the first tramcar up on Sunday morning (Welsh Industrial and Maritime Museum)

(above) *Central Hall, Tonypandy . . . this is just how I remember the 'Pandy of the 1920s with the Central Hall, founded by my grandfather, dominating the town. It was here that I first heard some of the great orators of the time and began to learn for myself the art of public speaking* (Welsh Industrial and Maritime Museum)

Just a memory . . . Bute East Dock, Cardiff, 1923. It was still fairly busy but even then the boom times were over, to return briefly during the 1939–45 war when the docks were pressed into service to transport much-needed coal for the war effort (Welsh Industrial and Maritime Museum)

The morning after . . . Dunraven Street, Tonypandy, November 1910, after the Tonypandy riots which were centred round the pit strike. Even in the angry hours, appearances are not neglected (Welsh Industrial and Maritime Museum)

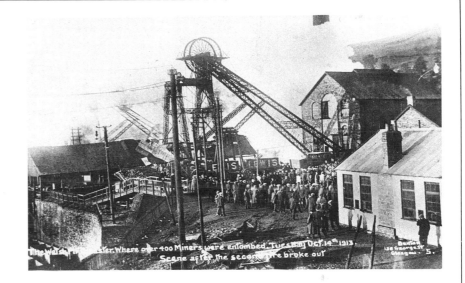

(above) *Disaster at Senghennydd . . . the worst disaster in the history of British coal mining took place on Tuesday 14 October 1913, at the Universal Colliery, Senghennydd. An explosion ripped through the mine killing 439 men and boys. The first picture shows the pit head scene after a second fire broke out and the second photograph shows the removal of the first bodies. Even now, nearly 75 years later, the people of Wales have not forgotten Senghennydd* (Welsh Folk Museum)

(left) *A pit at work . . . as a boy, this was a common sight throughout the valleys. I remember this pit particularly well; it's the Llwynypia mine belonging to the Glamorgan collieries where my stepfather, Dad Tom, worked in the winding house. Tonypandy and Clydach Vale are in the background* (Welsh Industrial and Maritime Museum)

All in a row . . . the houses in Clydach Vale clinging to the hillside of mid-Rhondda in the 1930s are very similar to the houses built at the turn of the century by my grandfather, John Tilbury, after his move to Tonypandy from Hampshire (Welsh Industrial and Maritime Museum)

CHAPTER ONE

OF COAL
AND
LEARNING

The enchantment of Wales lies as much in the patchwork of its scenery, its lakes, its mountains, its valleys, as it does in the equally varied characteristics of its people – north, south, east and west. The Celts are the founding fathers of the United Kingdom and as A. L. Rowse wrote, 'one of the joys of inhabiting an old country is that it is felt deep in the achievement of centuries, of memories, of associations'. In no part of the United Kingdom is this more true than it is in Wales where our hills and valleys endure as custodians of our past.

Over in south-west Wales, the old county of Pembrokeshire, which the planners have chosen to make part of Dyfed, has a unique charm with its gentle scenery matched by old world courtesy and kindness invariably revealed in conversation. The north of the county is Welsh speaking and fiercely proud of its Celtic heritage, while the south revels in its description as 'little England'. It was in Pembroke Castle that Harry Tudor, later to become King Henry VII, was born, the son of a fourteen-year-old girl who could not have known that her baby son would be the founder of the Tudor Dynasty. Perhaps I should not say it, but Pembrokeshire is very close to being my favourite county in Wales.

History can be found in every village, castles abound, each dripping with historical significance. And for me Wales' greatest jewel is St David's Cathedral, built on one of the very earliest Christian settlements in the whole of Britain. The sheer majesty of the remains of the Bishop's Palace standing cheek by jowl with the cathedral, reputedly founded by St David in the sixth century, brought tears to my eyes when I first saw it so many years ago. The thought of all the many Christian pilgrims whose prayers have been heard there through fourteen centuries makes my blood tingle. So many of the places have, like Dylan Thomas's Laugharne, defeated the ravages of time. It is hard indeed not to be moved by Pembrokeshire.

But each of the counties has a special place in my heart. Carmarthenshire (also part of Dyfed) is the home of my father's family and the knowledge that Carmarthenshire blood flows in my veins is still supreme. Overwhelmingly the language used in everyday affairs is Welsh – good Welsh, not Anglicized as it is in most parts of Glamorgan and Gwent. The language is genuinely used, not worn as a political badge. Carmarthenshire too has its ancient castles that keep our history alive. Kidwelly, for example, famous for its splendid castle dating back almost to the Conquest, has a town charter received from King John. One is constantly reminded of Carmarthenshire in churches throughout the world when the congregations stand to sing 'Guide me, O thou great Jehovah', for the hymn is the work of William Williams (1717–91) of Pantycelin, near Llandovery. As a Carmarthenshire man, Williams, probably the greatest hymn writer to come from Wales, naturally wrote in Welsh but his hymns have undoubtedly survived the translation into English.

Cardiganshire (yet again part of Dyfed) rightly boasts that it provided the home for Wales' first University College at Aberystwyth. A sparsely populated county, it too is rich in history and a veritable fortress of nonconformity. The joke that there are more sheep than people in Cardiganshire has probably more truth than humour! Small hillside farms have meant that the 'Cardis', as the local people are affectionately called, have had to be hard working and thrifty. The county joins with Montgomeryshire and Breconshire (both a part of Powys) to form mid-Wales which is regarded with equal affection by the people from the South and North, perhaps because in the Welsh language, Montgomeryshire is called the 'warm hearted county'. Newtown, the second largest town in the county, has long been a place of pilgrimage for Labour supporters in Wales who travel there to visit the grave of Robert Owen, the social and industrial reformer of the nineteenth century.

Social and religious reform seem to go hand in hand in Wales, and in the neighbouring county of Breconshire is Trefecca, the birthplace of Howell Harris, who, with the Wesleys and George Whitefield, played such an important role in the eighteenth-century religious revival. His remains rest in the fourteenth-century churchyard in Talgarth, Breconshire. Mid-Wales seems to me to have been more heavily influenced than the rest of Wales by the various religious orders which had their monasteries and churches securely established there for at least three centuries before the Reformation, whereas the north of the country has an altogether more rugged feel.

On a mountain overlooking the gorgeous Vale of Llangollen are clearly to be seen the remains of Castell Dinas Bran, the ancient home of Welsh princes in the North. Today these castle remains look down on Llangollen's International Eisteddfod which attracts competitors from right around the world. It is strange to think that Castell Dinas Bran housed Welsh soldiers many centuries before Columbus was sent by Isabella of Spain to look for the New World, or before John Cabot set sail from Bristol on his world travels. Every year now Llangollen is a magnet that draws singers and dancers from all the five continents.

History truly does have a habit of repeating itself. From 1201, when Madog ap Gruffydd, a prince of Powys, founded Valle Crucis Abbey in Llangollen for the Cistercian monks, right up to the Reformation, the area was a centre of religious culture and learning. Whenever I visit North Wales I am reminded that the more the world changes, the more it stays the same. The modern International Eisteddfod at Llangollen is history's echo of the singing of the monks in Valle Crucis Abbey. The monks would probably not have approved of the Ladies of Llangollen, Lady Eleanor Butler and Miss Sarah Ponsonby, two eighteenth-century eccentrics ahead of their time in female liberation. Their home was a tourist attraction even then. They had eloped together, and summoned men of distinction to their black and white house, Plas Newydd, demanding tributes, particularly carved pieces of oak, although William Wordsworth offered a sonnet. They and their maid, Molly the Basher, are buried near the river bank of St Collen's Parish Church.

Llangollen has a magnificent fourteenth-century stone bridge over the Dee and one of my favourite drives is through the Vale of Llangollen. The 46-mile long Llangollen Canal which flows into the valley of the Dee begins from its parent water, the Shropshire Union, at Hurleston and twists along until reaching a point where Thomas Telford's engineering gave it a more direct path. Today the Dee at Llangollen is a favourite white water course of canoeists where International Slalom and Rapid River events are held.

The whole of North Wales is interlaced with reminders of the turbulence of Welsh history. The unsurpassed grandeur of Snowdonia is matched by the apparently eternal castles at Flint, Rhuddlan, Dolwyddelan, Conwy, Denbigh, Caernarfon, Harlech and Beaumaris. Some of the castles are as overpowering in their majesty as are Snowdonia's mountain peaks. The Llanberis Pass must be one of the loveliest drives in Wales. It is here above lakes Padarn and Peris that Europe's largest pumped water storage scheme has been built, but cleverly hidden deep in the hills. You have to look hard at the grey-blue slate hills to see any evidence of its immense size, because most of it is buried in the Elidir mountain. You can take an easy walk up to Snowdon's summit or ride on the Llanberis Lake Railway, laid on the trackbed of a former slate quarry railway and which takes you along the eastern shores of Llyn Padarn. But the Pass can so easily change its face, and whenever I drive through it I have an overwhelming feeling that the mountains on either side are trying to close in on me. It is an especially frightening experience to be caught on the high mountain passes when either fog or snow darken the sky. When the darkness does fall it is easy to put yourself back thousands of years to imagine the ancient Welsh fighting for their land and their honour, but by no means all the great fortresses were built to guard the passes in the mountains of North Wales. A chain of castles was created near the old line of Offa's Dyke to guard the English border – even then we were trying to take over. Caerphilly Castle in mid-Glamorgan is the second largest open castle in Europe and played a major part in the seventeenth-century Civil War. Cromwell's men tried to destroy it but succeeded only in creating a sloping tower to rival the world-famous leaning tower of Pisa.

Right across the south, the remains of ancient abbeys and churches tell their own story. Cistercian abbey walls at Tintern in Gwent or at Neath in West Glamorgan match those at Valle Crucis. What superb architects and builders the Cistercian and Benedictine monks were! By building their great monasteries to the glory of God they placed succeeding generations in their debt. It is unfortunate, to say the least, that King Henry VIII's greed led to the despoliation of the abbeys and monasteries, thus cheating following generations of their rightful heritage. I suppose we should count our blessings that ancient cathedrals such as those at Llandaff, St David's and St Asaph were spared the ravages suffered by those which remained loyal to the Pope. Nimble footwork by church leaders (who enjoy an unswerving instinct for survival) ensured the protection of the glorious cathedrals dotted across the whole of England and Wales.

The magnetism of modern Wales encompasses much more than ancient buildings and ancient writings, significant though these are. Industrial South Wales had a vital role to play in the Industrial Revolution which made the United Kingdom the greatest power in the world. The coal, iron and steel industry in

(overleaf) *At the end of a shift . . . a South Wales miner washes off the grime of a day underground. I remember so well my mother telling me how the miners resisted the introduction of baths at the pithead as they feared being infested by fleas from their colleagues. The clothes pegs were fitted far enough apart to prevent fleas jumping from one man's jacket to another!*

South Wales attracted an enormous number of immigrants from both Ireland and from southern and south-west England, which was the home of my mother's parents before they came to Tonypandy. Social and cultural consequences arising from this mass immigration to South Wales still make themselves felt in the political and religious life of the Principality.

*

My eyes first opened in Port Talbot in 1909 but I didn't see much because our family moved back to the Rhondda when I was about two years old and it was there my eyes began to recognize people and places. It was there I learnt my perspective on life, which owes so much to my mother and my brothers and sisters.

My grandparents John and Elizabeth Tilbury had come to the Rhondda Valley in 1872 from their home in Hampshire, drawn by the Industrial Revolution to what they saw as the booming coal industry that was to power Britain's future, at sea and on the rails. They originally opened a greengrocer's in Tonypandy but my grandfather soon saw the potential in the large numbers of people moving into the Valley, where more and more new pits were being sunk, and became a builder of houses for them. A year after I was born, there were fifty-six coal mines in the Rhondda. Now there is one.

My mother, Emma Jane, known to us children – and later to practically everybody in the Labour Party and the House of Commons – as 'Mam', was born on 12 January 1881. Against her parents' wishes she married the first boy she went out with, a young miner called Zachariah Thomas from Carmarthen who barely spoke English.

They were married in Pontypridd in 1900 when they were both nineteen, in the Church in Wales, because the English Methodist Chapel, founded by my grandfather and another English immigrant, John Hearn, had not yet received a licence for weddings. The family soon grew: Ada May was born in 1902, Dolly in 1904, Emrys in 1906, me in January 1909 and Ivor in December of the same year.

The fact that Ivor and I were born so close together meant that my mother had a very severe burden to carry wherever she went. She used to tell me that she would put us both in the pram and push it all the way to Margam Abbey, about a four-mile walk from Port Talbot. We were apparently content in the pram.

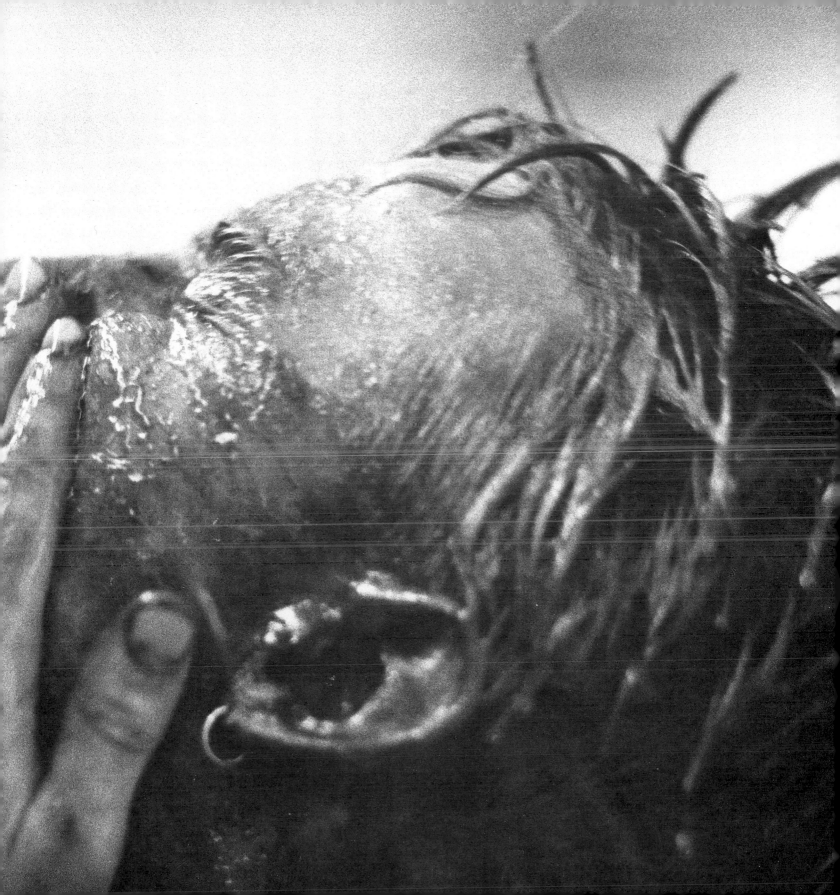

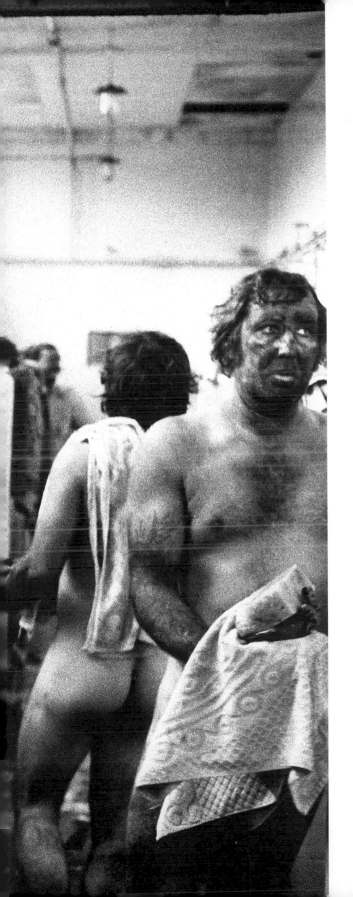

I remember very little of Port Talbot but I do recall waiting by the side of the main Cardiff to Swansea road while a train passed by. I must have been very young because I was in school in Penygraig back near Tonypandy when I was only two and a half. The teacher there had taken pity on my mother with two such young children and had allowed me to start early.

There is little else I know about my time at Port Talbot except that I was carried into the Methodist Chapel and christened. About twenty-five years ago when I was preaching in the chapel in Tydraw Street, opposite the house where I was born, I said that I had been christened there. Without me realizing it, the minister

(left) *The last pit in the Rhondda . . . these are probably the last of the South Wales miners who for so many years were the pride of the Rhondda.*
(right) *A little piece of history . . . as small boys my brother Ivor and I were used to seeing the coal-stained faces of the miners returning home – something most children of the Rhondda now will never have seen.*

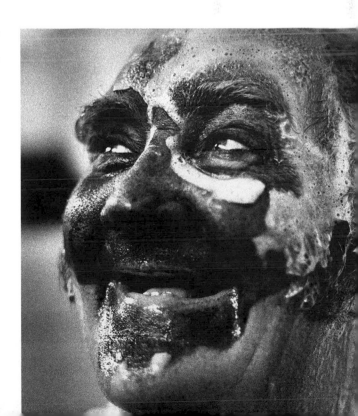

went to the vestry to look up his old christening book and to be sure there he found the name of Thomas George Thomas, son of Zachariah and Emma Jane Thomas, so I feel very close to that chapel.

The people of Port Talbot have been very good to me. Ivor Williams, a man whose life was shared between chapel and sport, and who lived to be nearly ninety, took the lead in the last year of his life – 1984 – to ensure that a plaque was put outside the house where I was born. The few years my parents lived in Port Talbot were very difficult for my mother. It was there my father started drinking and it was then that her mother died. My mother told me of her last visit. She went from Port Talbot to Tonypandy by train through the tunnel under the mountain at the top of the Rhondda valley. As she was coming down to Tonypandy station she looked to their house and saw the blinds were all drawn. That told her she was too late – her mother was dead.

On our return to Penygraig we lived in Hughes Street. They were not happy times. On the outbreak of the First World War my father enlisted at once. We never saw him again. During his army service he met another woman and began a new life in Kent.

The six of us had to move from our home to an underhouse, a basement flat, in Miskin Road, Trealaw. For a time my mother's Aunt Maria – a real tartar – lived next door to us. It was my job to light her fire each morning before going to school. I used to carry in a bucket of coal and firewood, and clean out the grate while she sat upright in bed looking rather like Queen Victoria. She had a tongue as sharp as a razor, and would direct a stream of criticism at me, particularly objecting if I used more than four pieces of wood at a time – even though we provided both the coal and the sticks!

Much earlier, when Aunt Maria and her husband George lived further away, he always used to take home one of Grandma's apple tarts after visiting her, because Aunt Maria said she could not eat bought ones. He once forgot to take his tart, so he went to the shop for one. Aunt Maria thoroughly enjoyed it, but when he admitted two weeks later it had been from a shop, she was promptly sick!

On Thursday mornings, Mam used to go to Miskin Road Post Office to collect Aunt Maria's pension of 5s; everyone called it Lloyd George Money, because he was the Chancellor of the Exchequer who had introduced the pensions, and we marvelled when it was raised to 7s 6d.

A man of Maerdy . . . dressed for work, a miner at Maerdy Colliery, the last pit in the Rhondda. Since I was a boy, more than 50 coal mines have closed. After 30 June 1986 no more coal was brought to the surface in the Rhondda.

(overleaf) *Divided loyalties . . . these Cardiff school children are playing by the railings at Ninian Park, home of Cardiff City Football Club. Despite Wales' devotion to rugby football, Cardiff City has always had a special place in the affections of the principality's capital. Only the die-hards persist in referring to soccer as 'the wrong code'.*

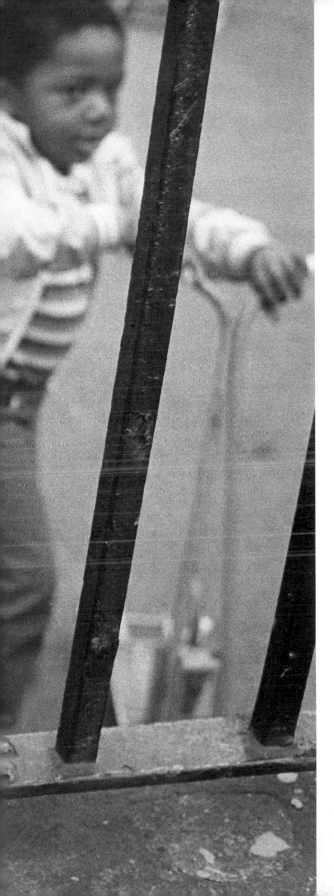

Like all small children, particularly in such an isolated place as the Rhondda – actually two valleys, Rhondda Fawr (large) and Rhondda Fach (small) – we thought that where we lived was the entire world. We were not conscious of the life outside.

My first understanding of Wales and being Welsh came one St David's Day at Trealaw Boys' School when I was about eight. We all took part in a play showing the history of Wales. I played Owain Glyndŵr, the fourteenth-century Welsh prince and a great fighter who unified Wales and whose burial place is just outside Brecon. Owain Glyndŵr had an enormous influence on the whole of Wales but especially remembered are his achievements in Sycharth Castle which he had established not far to the south west of Oswestry. Nothing of the castle itself has survived the erosion of time but it is Montgomeryshire's proud boast that in Machynlleth there still stands the building that housed his Welsh Parliament. The Parliament itself disappeared with Glyndŵr but the building still serves as a source of inspiration for those in Wales who yearn for the independence he dreamed of. I suppose that those who in the past two decades have been setting fire to the holiday homes bought and modernized by English people believe they are following in his steps. Nothing could be further from the truth: Glyndŵr showed courage, whereas these arsonists reveal only cowardice by acting in lonely unsupervised places and sneaking away in the dark.

When we at school marked St David's Day, it was a genuine celebration of being Welsh. The children would each represent a county in Wales and recite a poem about it.

It was the day of the year when we sang the Welsh folk songs – usually in English because even then the Rhondda was greatly Anglicized. We also used to wear a leek on our jackets and we would always nibble at it. Legend says the Welsh and English were having one of their inevitable battles, neither side wearing distinctive uniform, in a field where leeks were growing. The Welsh soldiers picked some leeks and wore them so they would know who was on their side. But now the daffodil, the national flower of Wales, seems, perhaps for obvious reasons, to be replacing the leek as the national emblem of Wales. But it has less impact somehow. The leek is more aggressive, more in tune with the dragon. For we boys in Trealaw the daffodil would not have seemed manly enough. We were a very fierce bunch and grew up in a very Old Testament atmosphere. Even the names came from

35

the Old Testament: Jeremiah, Isaiah, Zachariah and Obadiah were common.

There was not then a great sense of nationalism and St David's Day was the only day of the year when we laid a specific emphasis on the fact that we were Welsh. We were different; the English had never conquered us. And there *is* something special about the Welsh.

By and large the Welsh-speaking Welshman is even more conscious of his difference from the Saxons. The true Celts, even if some of them have English fathers, would claim to be descended from the Celts who were forced out of England 2000 years ago. Just to grow up in the Valley is to have the feeling of Wales and the pride in Wales, the depth of friendship, the joy of conversation and the love of music which is our natural heritage.

No one consciously teaches the young to harmonize; it is something caught from one's playmates. Many, many times I would start singing and one of my friends would join in with a marvellous harmony. We never thought this to be anything out of the ordinary, but we enjoyed it. Once we started singing we would go on for an hour or more. We were never taught how to do it and it cannot be explained.

The Welsh are also marked out by a particular brand of humour, often gently mocking, sometimes macabre. Throughout my youth one well-known miners' leader and local preacher in mid-Rhondda was universally referred to as 'Dai Bomb'. I simply could not understand why, so finally I asked my mother to explain. Hardly believing I could be so stupid, she said: 'Surely you have heard him speak, George? His full name is Dai Bombastic!' Two other local men were known respectively as 'Dai Bungalow' and 'Dai Six Months' – the first because he was not very bright so had nothing upstairs, the other because he had lost half an ear in an accident!

The people found it possible to joke in times of distress. If there had been an accident underground a miner would be sent to the man's home to break the news. The story sticks in my mind of the man who went and said: 'Is Mrs Jones the widow living here?' She replied, 'I'm Mrs Jones, I'm not a widow.' 'Oh yes you are,' he said. How cruel that sounds but perhaps that sort of barbed humour helped them cope. Life was cheap in the valleys in the early years of this century. Fatal accidents in the pits were commonplace, so the somewhat grisly sense of humour was probably an accepted form of escapism.

Perhaps the characteristics of the Welsh have a lot to do with the sheer isolation of valley life right up to the Second World War. Each valley has its own characteristics and until about twenty-five years ago, I could still tell the difference in the accents of a Rhondda man, a Merthyr Valley man and an Aberdare man.

It is amazing how in those valleys people who never had more than an elementary school education became great orators. This is surely another natural gift. I think back to those old miners' leaders of Tonypandy who really characterized Wales for me (most of them as it happened only English speaking); how well read they were, and how I admired their insatiable eagerness to learn. Remember too, that most of them had left school at ten to go down the pits after passing the Labour Examination to see that they could read and write. There were no physical tests at all.

By the time my brother Emrys went down Llwynypia mine the Labour Examination had gone and the age limit raised to thirteen. From the moment he started, he always gave my mother his pay: it was Emrys who kept me out of the pit and on at school. It was the great ambition of all the parents to keep at least their youngest sons out of the pit and it was accepted that the elder son would help support his brothers. Yet, those of us who did not go down were jealous of those who did because they were the men. We felt that they were manly, as they told the rest of us stories of what went on underground.

We loved the stories but were all a bit frightened of even the thought of going down in the cage. I have been down since, of course, and it is the strangest sensation. When you are about half way down you get the impression you are going back up. The boys may have exaggerated, but it was tough down there.

For safety reasons the underground roadways were divided by heavy doors, and it was particularly dangerous for the door boys who had to push them open when the trucks loaded with coal came racing along. There used to be a long line of these trucks and each miner would put his initials in chalk on his own truck because the amount and the grade of coal determined how much a man would be paid. Some men, either carelessly or deliberately, would throw in some stone with the coal, so it was important to identify your own load.

Once at the top the load was washed and weighed, and because the men thought the management was liable to cheat, they insisted

Folk art . . . the faded tile mural of a Welsh dragon pretending to be bold, at the entrance to the Boys' Village at St Athan, originally set up by the Ocean Colliery Company Recreation Association to provide holidays for the sons of miners.

(above) *Lunchtime in Wales One . . . a couple take lunch in their car sheltering from the cold overlooking the beach at Llantwit Major where my mother learned to walk again.*

(left) *Lunchtime in Wales Two . . . a school crossing patrol lady snatches a few minutes to read on the steps of her school before shepherding the future of Wales across the road. Trealaw School, where I learnt to read and write; in my day, we only had to dodge the horses!*

(overleaf) *The future . . . children of Tonypandy eat their sweets after school near Primrose Hill, the site of the old water mill which gave Tonypandy its name and where my mother was born.*

that their own check-weighers were employed to see there was justice done to the men who were working below. It was really the first productivity deal and the beginnings of an organized workforce to take on the colliery owners.

There is in Wales a strong neighbourliness amongst its people; there is an unfailing loyalty one for the other, that is not always found elsewhere. Nowhere was that more evident than amongst the miners who kept an eye out for each other and the boys who worked alongside them and who were the sons of their friends. Underground was a hard place to be, tempers sometimes frayed and a man could easily give way to crueller instincts.

The one thing that the miners used to watch particularly was any bullying of the young boys, and they would fiercely attack those who bullied the youngsters. The bullies were additionally punished by the fact that their misbehaviour was the one underground secret that was allowed to come out. People would soon know if a man was a bully underground, and once that was known he would find it difficult to get a boy working with him because the pit management would hear and not allocate anybody to him. It would then be very difficult for him to work at all, as each miner would need to have a boy with him to work as a team at the face. The man would dig the coal and the boy put it in the wagon for the surface.

Those days have gone now and children in the Rhondda of the Eighties have no idea what miners looked like when they came home from work with their blackened faces. I used to see them flocking like people going to a football match with their 'Tommy' box, a tin for sandwiches which they had to keep from the rats underground. They usually carried a bottle of water or cold tea.

These then are the places and the men who fashioned my life, men who lived through the long Cambrian Combine Strike of 1910, the year after I was born. Memories of it still live on as the stories are passed down from miner to miner. Its causes and effects are still well known in the Rhondda today, but when I was a young man, the leaders of that strike were then in their forties and leaders of both chapel and council. Their memories were still fresh, their influence enormous.

The trouble had begun in pricing wages for a new seam in the Ely pit of the Naval Colliery Company. The company offered 1s 9d a ton while the men wanted 2s 6d because it was going to be particularly difficult work. The two sides failed to reach agree-

ment, and on 1 September 1910 the company locked out not only the fifty or so men directly involved but the entire 800 men at Ely, which in turn led to a strike throughout the Welsh coalfield.

The Cambrian Combine Strike began on 1 November and within a week 12,000 miners were out in the Rhondda and 11,000 in Aberdare. Eventually, 30,000 miners were either on strike or locked out. Feelings rose high over the plan to bring non-striking miners into the pits, particularly in Tonypandy where there were demonstrations and fights with the police.

Perhaps overreacting, the Chief Constable of Glamorgan asked for troops to be sent in and spoke on the telephone to Winston Churchill, then the Home Secretary in a Liberal government. The Tonypandy Rebellion became a national issue. Churchill never forgot it. Even in 1945 when he came to Cardiff to launch his General Election campaign, his speech was devoted to clearing his name. He said he never sent the troops to Tonypandy, that he had halted them at Swindon. He was not concerned with the election: he thought that was in his pocket. He was wrong on both counts. The troops were held up for only twenty-four hours and he lost the election with the Labour landslide. But in fairness one has to admit that a Labour Home Secretary at that time would probably have behaved in the same way once the police proved ineffective in controlling the rioters.

There were many things that happened in the 1983–4 miners' strike that should not have happened but there were still similarities with the Welsh strike of 1910. The hostile attitude to the police may have started then, although it was always said that the local bobbies behaved properly; it was the outsiders who brought the trouble with them. The women too were crucial to the 1910 strikes. If the women caught a strike-breaker they would humiliate him by putting a white shirt over his head – the ultimate disgrace.

The people of Tonypandy had to wait only sixteen years before they were again hit by a major strike, which this time lasted nine months. The General Strike of 1926 spread hardship and misery throughout the valleys. The miners and their younger brothers would collect coal by candlelight from the caves in the valleys and the women would organize the soup kitchen.

The strikers and their families were getting consistently poorer all the time and could not afford to buy a new suit or repair their shoes, which were stuffed with brown paper. This inability to dress smartly had a cultural consequence, for these people took a pride in keeping a best suit to go to chapel. They believed that if you were going to worship God then you should go in your best. Therefore they began to stay away from chapel and congregations fell. It was cruel, for the chapel had been their life and yet they stayed away because they were ashamed. And there was no other work available for them to earn money.

We had a slogan: 'Don't send people to the work, bring the work to the people'. Our heritage is the community itself which cannot exist without roots. Today the government needs to learn that lesson yet again. It is not enough to say, 'Leave your community and find work' – capital can move more easily than people. I will never forget the regular Monday morning scene at Tonypandy station when groups of crying young people, the sons and daughters of miners, would be off to London or Birmingham to find work. But they took their politics with them and were eventually to change the face of Britain in 1945 when the old guard was toppled from power. The Establishment was made to pay the price of the Depression. They may yet have to do so again.

During the General Strike we were living in 201 Trealaw Road where we had moved in 1925 after Mam had married Tom Davies, a safety man at Llywnypia pit. We were much better off than the other eighty per cent of our chapel who were hit by the strike because 'Dad Tom', as I called him, continued to work. The miners agreed to the safety men going in so that their jobs would be saved when the strike finally finished. They all wanted a job afterwards, but they realized that if the pit was flooded, it and all of them would be finished.

Dad Tom was very relieved to be at work and I suppose there must have been some envious people but it never showed to me nor, I think, to my mother who was caught up with the soup kitchen. Money was raised in collections, all around the country, and the Lord Mayor of London, Sir William Pryke, set up a Relief Fund, for there were only ha'pennies to be had in the valleys.

The two Rhondda valleys with their twenty villages had a total population of 180,000, more than 40,000 of whom were working miners. The plight of the women and children during the long strike was particularly pitiful – the Rhondda Urban District Council requiring at least £1500 a week in order to supply milk to expectant mothers and young babies. More than 40,000 applications for relief of destitute persons in Pontypridd alone were dealt with by the local board of guardians. Under the Feeding of Necessitous School Children Act, youngsters were lined up in school kitchens for one meal a day.

The contribution made by the people of Tonypandy, apart from the soup kitchens, was really in keeping the men entertained; remember, these were healthy young men roaming around and there was very little trouble. There were, of course, the constraints of religion and a natural sense of discipline, but everyone also made sure that the energy of these young people was used, and football matches – not rugby – were organized on a big scale. If the same thing happened now, rugby would be played – a sport which has become such a part of Wales, and so linked with national pride.

The older character of the valley, which I fear is fading, was hewn out of the isolation, the need to depend on each other, and the sharing of the same experiences, which usually involved at least some form of hardship.

The people were bound together too by the regular threat of bad news from the pit. One of the things that would horrify people was the unexpected sound of the pit hooter which was normally used only to mark the change of shifts. We knew when it shrieked its alarm out of time that there had been major trouble. The whole community would know something was up but would not know which families were involved, so everybody who had men down the pit left their houses to gather at the pit head. The toll in South Wales was particularly heavy: between 1850 and 1920, 3179 miners died, and from 1890 to 1913 there were thirteen disasters. Among the major tragedies was Senghennydd in 1913 which claimed 439 lives.

I still remember vividly one night in the 1930s when I was home from University College, Southampton, where I was on a teacher training course. We heard the hooter at the Llwynypia pit where Dad Tom was working. He was duty winder that night; he had lowered the men who were now trapped below. He also lowered the rescuers. Twelve men died that night and I remember later going to the top of the mountain to watch the two-mile long funeral procession snaking its way to the cemetery. There had in earlier years been far worse disasters but it somehow hurts more when it is, as it were, your own pit.

CHAPTER TWO

OF CHURCHES AND CHAPELS

There is no question that the biggest single influence on the Wales I grew up in was the chapel. Nearly everybody went, and there was such a choice – everything was duplicated simply on the grounds of language. Where there was a Welsh-speaking chapel there was also one for the English speakers, often only a hundred yards apart. It was a time of great luxury for religion if not for the congregations.

That remained the case right up to 1940, long after I had started preaching. I remember a place called Ferndale in Rhondda Fach where there was a Welsh and an English Methodist chapel in the same street, yet the congregations did not know each other. I used to preach in the English chapel and the people in the Welsh one were total strangers to me. We just never met.

Today things have changed and the English and Welsh speakers find it possible to worship together. They have a hymn in Welsh – everyone can sing Welsh – together with a reading or prayer in Welsh but the sermon is usually in English, because otherwise the great majority would not be able to follow it. Even a Welsh-speaking preacher will throw liberal doses of English into his sermon.

Wales and Methodism are linked in a very special way. It was George Whitefield from Gloucester, who was ordained 250 years ago, who really converted Wales, not John Wesley. Whitefield was a friend of both John and Charles Wesley and they both owed a great deal to his influence. A dynamic preacher, like the Wesleys, he was a leader of the great eighteenth-century religious revival. In harmony with the Wesleys, he spent many years in America. He and Wesley agreed to disagree on the Calvinist doctrines, so they each went their own way. Whitefield formed the Presbyterian movement in Wales which the Welsh tend to call Methodist. Whitefield is not given the credit he deserves, largely because of the huge reputation Wesley built up. Wesley spent less time in Wales than Whitefield, but he did come on horseback a few times to preach in South Wales, then a rural area with just a few lonely villages. I'm sure he used to exaggerate the size of his congregations but he was undoubtedly an inspired leader. When he could, Wesley used to stay in the best places for he liked his comfort, but he always rose between half past four and five in the morning for a time of prayer before going to his next appointment. The Wesleys and Whitefield left a thriving network of chapels in Wales. Their influence was to be found everywhere. A story recounted by

This pleasant land . . . south of Bethesda near Penrhyn Slate Quarry.

(overleaf) *A break in the cloud . . . the sun acts as a spotlight on the clifftop at Porth Colmon.*

(above) *Beached . . . waiting the tide on the Lleyn Peninsula.*

(left) *Changing shades . . . Gwydyr Forest in the greens and browns of autumn.*

(overleaf) *The majesty of Snowdonia . . . Llyn Padarn and Llanberis Pass.*

(above) *A trick of light . . . rays from a watery sun break through near Pwllheli.*

(right) *Trees to the skyline . . . a hillside near Nantmor.*

(overleaf) *The pride of Wales . . . Snowdon, beloved of serious climbers and weekend walkers alike. The 1953 Everest expedition did their training here.*

*Unchanging style . . . the Post Office and village stores at Nant-Gwynant,
much as they always have been.*

Emrys Pride in his book *Rhondda My Valley Brave* tells of the rescue of a group of miners who, in April 1877, were trapped for eleven days by flood and fallen stone in the Tynewydd pit. When they were finally rescued they were found singing hymns as they had been throughout their ordeal. Love of hymn singing is at the very heart of nonconformist Wales.

The valleys' faith probably goes back to the ancient Celts who were also deeply religious; certainly Wales for centuries seemed more religious than England. Celtic people are less afraid of emotion than are the English. The English public school tradition of people having an iron control over their emotions under all circumstances has little appeal for the Wales in which I was nurtured. Heaven knows, the successive cruel pit disasters to which Wales was subject for about a hundred years stirred deep and powerful emotions.

It was the chapels, always radical while the Church was regarded as the voice of the Establishment, that played a major part in the education and cultural life of the country. There was a high rate of literacy and the chapel leaders saw education as the key to everything. These people, nearly all of them with only the most basic formal education, would read everything they could lay their hands on. history, philosophy, poetry and science. Shakespeare was often quoted in political speeches, as of course was Charles Dickens.

Attendance at school was strictly controlled in my time as a pupil. We were all frightened by the truancy officer, or the school whipper-in as we called him. He was employed to go around looking for any child walking about the streets who ought to be in school. I dealt with him personally only once, because I liked going to school. One day I had been up to see my father's mother who could not speak English and as I came out of the back of the house I was face to face with the whipper-in. He was very fierce. He accepted my story that I was visiting my grandmother, but I never remember missing school again.

At that time too, you would have the cane if you were absent from school without just cause. And it would hurt, making your fingers swell. I received the cane on just one occasion when a large number of us were caned together. Some of the older boys goaded me into going home to mother. She was not impressed; she caught hold of me and marched me back to school where I had to go in shame-faced. I had no sympathy from the boys either!

(above) *Nature takes over . . . ivy conquers a gravestone in Llanover Church, Gwent, where earthly remains crumble.*

(right) *So peaceful . . . Vaynor Old Parish Church, the final resting place of the Crawshay dynasty who lived at Cyfartha Castle in Merthyr. The grave of Robert Thompson Crawshay, the last of the line to live in the castle, bears the inscription: 'God forgive me'.*

My other brush with authority came when I was very young and had gone with my younger brother Ivor and some of the other boys to Dunraven Street, Tonypandy. We wandered down Kenry Street to the bottom of Primrose Hill – another lovely name which tells you what the town used to be like – where there was a bookshop with books outside on a stall. One of the boys encouraged me to take one and I took it home. My mother, naturally angry, told me that that was stealing and I should take the book back. When I got to the shop the local bobby, Bobby Jones, who was in Tonypandy for years, was there. The fear of offending my mother was greater than the fear of him so in I went. He read me the riot act. That was a very important lesson – I couldn't have been much more than five or six – for it shows how easily a child can get into trouble. I am sure that the bookseller would not have missed that book amongst all the others but I had to go through a great deal of misery in confessing what I had done. I did not know then that I was too young to be prosecuted!

I really did love it at Tonypandy Higher Grade School, later to become Tonypandy Grammar and now Tonypandy Comprehensive. We had no school meals but took sandwiches for our lunch and had coffee from a big urn. There was a boy there called Walter Lock, a brilliant boy who we all knew was what we then called a love-child. He was cleverer than any of us and he was full of mischief. One lunch time when we went to have our coffee we soon discovered that someone had put soap in the urn. The headmaster, Mr Hawkins, summoned the whole school to say we would be kept in for half an hour every day until the culprit owned up. Walter held out for three days but then this little fellow, like George Washington – 'I cannot tell a lie' – said: 'Sir, I did it.' His honesty cost him the cane before the whole school. His mischief earned him the admiration of the rest of us. I have often thought that in the privacy of the Staff Common Room there must have been some hearty laughter about the incident.

Every Christmas there was a school concert and we had to register our names in early October if we were willing to participate. The previous July at our chapel anniversary I had recited Kipling's 'If' and I volunteered to repeat the performance. In December when the concert came I had forgotten my name was there. The headmaster called out: 'George Thomas, Form 1A, to recite "If".' I just managed to say 'If' and had eventually to go back to my seat without saying even the first line! I never put my name down for anything after that, without making sure that I had it all right.

Our school had a little concrete yard where I learned to play tennis. I remember pleading to be allowed a racquet of my own, and eventually had one for 7s 6d – the cheapest and the heaviest – on the market.

I have particular memories of one master at the school, Mr Jones, 'Froggie' the French teacher, who used to address me in a very superior way. He was the only teacher to call us by our surnames and in Wales it is insulting to call a man only by his surname, although in England nobody minds. He used to say, 'Thomas, you are the sort of person who will end up on Trinity Corner [a square in Tonypandy] with a bag of chips in one hand and a packet of Woodbines in the other!' Whenever he said it, I quivered, for I was eager to get on in life.

Many years later when I was an MP, I returned to Tonypandy Grammar School to present the prizes. Mr Jones was still teaching there and I reminded him of the story. He really believed I was going to use it in my speech, particularly when I told the boys what memories I had of Mr Jones, the French master. 'What did we call him?' I asked and the whole school yelled out 'Froggie' and I finished my memories there! I was not going to let him down. He was a good teacher and I have often thought how much I owe to him.

There were no playing fields for us but we would climb the mountain for a decent game of football. We knew every inch and every path which to the uninitiated was like trying to follow a sand track through a desert. We knew our mountains and we knew all the crevices where the earth split apart and from time to time trapped a sheep or a dog that had fallen down. On one occasion when about a dozen of us were going to play a game, we heard a dog barking at the bottom of a crevice. One of the boys went all the way back down the mountain to get a rope which we tied round the waist of my elder brother Emrys so we could lower him down the crack which was only just wide enough for him. My blood goes cold now as I realize the terrible risks we were taking, but that day Emrys rescued the dog as those of us at the top hauled on the rope dragging him back up. The story reminds me now both of the respect we had for animals and the complete lack of fear young children can have.

After school we would play football with a tin and put our coats

(overleaf) A special place . . . I have always thought of the Vale of Glamorgan as a place of unsurpassed beauty. It was here at Southerndown, near Ogmore-by-Sea, that Ivor and I drove with my mother as she regained the use of her legs.

down on the ground in the street to mark goal posts with one boy on the look-out for Bobby Jones. If he caught us, and he was a good runner, he would give us a thump, but nobody would dream of telling their parents or we would get another one from them. It was no good going home to complain because parents would say, 'You must have done something to deserve it', and punish you again. But those were the days when men and women in authority were supported, unlike today. I trace some of the current resentment of all authority to the brawling in Parliament. When people hear the rowdies trying to shout down a point of view they don't like, they may easily think that if such behaviour is parliamentary conduct, then it must be acceptable.

In a democracy, everybody must have the right to express their point of view. Everything that was taught us at school, in chapel and by our community leaders in the Rhondda, was to equip us to exercise this right, to develop our thoughts and to express them clearly. For my part I owe a special debt to Tom Smith, a miners' leader and local councillor who held a speakers' class at his home every Tuesday evening. I was one of four teenagers who regularly went to Tom Smith's house for instruction. He taught us logic and how to apply it in a speech. He showed us how to construct a speech and throughout my life I have followed Tom Smith's method. It's strange that this man had the urge to teach; we didn't pay him anything for it, but every Tuesday we would go to his home and have the oil lamp in the middle of the table while we argued about the best way to talk in public.

Tonypandy Central Hall, of which my grandfather was a founder trustee, became the centre of Rhondda life. I read the lesson at the official opening of the Hall and I gave the last sermon when it closed in 1981. The building was demolished in 1985 to make way for a shopping centre. But right up to the Second World War it would have an evening congregation of about eight hundred. People would queue round the block to get a good seat — at the services as well as the celebrity concerts which were a feature of the Central Hall in the years of the Depression. A season ticket cost 7s 6d which was a small fortune then, but the money was found somehow. All the great singers came down because they wanted to do something for the depressed areas. They knew also that they would always have an appreciative audience of a thousand music lovers.

Throughout the years of mass unemployment, the concerts, the

(above) *Blown away . . . the sails are missing from this windmill near Usk, in Gwent.*

(left) *Weathered glory . . . the intricate patterns on Llanover Church still survive. Among the worshippers at the church was Lady Llanover, a relation of Benjamin Hall who gave his name to Big Ben – my constant time-piece during my years as Speaker of the House of Commons.*

(Overleaf) *Hillside vigil . . . a cemetary overlooking Aberfan where generations of the townsfolk are buried on a hillside above.*

regular football matches and the chapel kept us occupied and there was very little crime. We never had a lock on our door and could go out without being worried in case we were burgled. It was an entirely different world from the one in which we live today where we have so many more things, yet the more we have, the more we seem to want.

It was in the Depression that another outlet for our energies was provided by William and Emma Noble, a Quaker couple, who opened a house called Maes-yr-Haf for all kinds of educational and recreational activities. Lecturers and students from Oxford and Cambridge came to lead the study groups. I did not know it at the time but one of the students who came was Henry Brooke, later to become Home Secretary in Harold Macmillan's government. Amongst the lecturers was Dorothy Emmett who ran philosophy classes at the Central Hall. There would be about forty in her men's class, of which I was the secretary. There was an enormous box of books which I had to distribute and then put back again to return to Oxford so that we could receive fresh supplies. There was an unquenchable thirst for knowledge with discussion groups of all kinds. Lively argument stirred the intellects of us all. We were the last generation before radio and, much later, television, brought drastic changes in the reading habits of the young.

Throughout my teenage years I felt pulled between the desire to be a teacher and the feeling that I was being called to the ordained Methodist ministry. When I was seventeen I became a pupil teacher at a local school where the headmaster was called 'Snow-drop' because he had round shoulders and a permanent stoop. I well remember the day he blew a whistle to summon the whole school into the yard. He pointed to the sky and for the first time we saw an aeroplane. Snowdrop told us: 'The time will come when people will travel around in those things', and none of us believed him. I decided to go ahead with my plans to become a teacher and went to University College, Southampton, where, because of my accent and background, I was given the nickname of Lord Tonypandy! Throughout my student days I continued to feel that I was being called to be an ordained minister, and this was finally resolved when Owen Buckley encouraged me to become a local preacher. Owen Buckley had been a very close friend of Mam's brother George, after whom I was named. Largely a self-educated man, he knew the Book of Psalms by heart and could reel off quotations from Burns, Wordsworth and

Tennyson. One Sunday night, after evening service, he said: 'I'm due to preach in Llwynypia next Sunday. You must come with me and read the lesson.'

It was impossible to refuse, but the following Sunday I was hit by nerves as I looked down from the pulpit to the congregation. They were all friends of mine, yet as I stood up and faced them I could hear my own voice quaver. When, after the second service, Owen Buckley said to me: 'You know that God is calling you to be a preacher, George, it is time that you responded', he echoed my own feelings.

Knowledge of the complete sermons of John Wesley was an essential requirement for anyone wishing to be recognized as a Methodist local preacher, and I set about studying them. Another was to preach a trial sermon, which I did one Tuesday evening at Treherbert Methodist chapel. The local preachers present to assess me included Owen Buckley, and it was intimidating to address the assembly of familiar men, nearly all of them miners, who had so much preaching experience between them. The people of the valleys were real 'sermon tasters' in those days. People would walk miles to hear a good preacher and then they would discuss the sermon with each other.

Becoming a local preacher meant a good deal of additional exercise for both mind and body. Many of the chapels I was sent to were quite a distance from Tonypandy, and there was not always enough money for the bus fare. One Sunday I was due to be in Treherbert Chapel, about eight miles up the valley, but had only threepence for the single fare. I decided I would go up in the bus, since that way I would be fresher for preaching, and then walk back.

But when we came out of the chapel, several people wanted to see me to the bus stop, and I didn't want them to know I had no money. So in order to shake them off, I decided to call on a friend nearby. I never minded walking; the early Methodists used to walk up to twenty miles to preach a sermon, and I was quite proud that I sometimes had to walk too.

The preparation of those early sermons was hard work. They were expected to last at least thirty-five minutes, and I would spend some of my evenings looking up Bible commentaries, reading the views of different people on particular passages, and then applying my own thoughts and imagination to making links with our lives in the Rhondda.

In those days we always called on our congregations for total commitment, for we were evangelists seeking recruits. I still am: I believe the main purpose of the Church is to proclaim the Gospel, and that it is for each individual to work out how to bring Christian principles to bear on modern issues. Amongst my reading was the work of the American theologian Harry Emerson Fosdick. His argument that we should see all men through the eyes of Our Lord, see them in terms of their possibilities once they have been transformed by the Holy Spirit, hit me like a hammer blow. I found it a short jump from that to imagining how under-privileged folk could develop into mighty men if their economic circumstances were improved and an even shorter jump to an increasingly active role in Labour Party politics. I followed in Mam's footsteps and was elected chairman of Tonypandy Ward Labour Party.

Alongside preaching and politics, I was also teaching at Marlborough Road School, Cardiff, and had become heavily involved in the National Union of Teachers. I used to travel from Tonypandy to Cardiff every day on a weekly season ticket that took 7s out of my £5 salary. We people on the train became a community of our own and everybody chatted freely until we reached Whitchurch station just outside Cardiff. Then we used to say we were in Tory Disneyland because nobody spoke to us – they would come in and not say a word. Sometimes one would have the cheek to open the window and then one of us would get up and close it. Then the war came and the barriers went down. We knew that we would sink or swim together; our destinies were interlocked. Everyone chatted freely.

I had joined the NUT when I was in college so I went to the meetings of the Cardiff Association of Teachers whenever I could. At my very first meeting motions for the NUT Conference were being selected. I wanted one condemning unemployment and calling on the government to take action. I made a fiery speech which I thought would disturb the meeting. Imagine my surprise when at the end of the meeting, I was elected to attend the NUT Conference in Portsmouth to represent the Cardiff teachers.

Thinking back, I realize that the Cardiff NUT members must have been a very tolerant crowd because I remember looking around the meeting and saying: 'It's all right for you to come here with your fur coats and your polished shoes, but you only have to go twenty miles away and people have not enough to eat.' In the arrogance of youth I had mistakenly believed that I cared for the unemployed more than the others did. They proved me wrong, but in a gracious way – by sending me to the conference.

It was the Nonconformists who reflected Welsh radicalism. That is changing now with the closing of so many chapels and the rising popularity of the Anglican church in Wales. Since it was disestablished in 1920, the Church in Wales has gone from strength to strength. There may be a moral there for the Church of England. Before disestablishment the Church in Wales was under very strong English domination which did not help its popularity. When disestablishment took place, the Church in Wales became more sturdy, with its own Archbishop and half-a-dozen bishops. Incidentally, the opportunities for promotion to higher Church offices increased in Wales almost overnight. It was the same when Harold Wilson set up the Welsh Office in 1964. There were about thirty Labour MPs from Wales, one of whom was guaranteed a seat in the Cabinet, and many others would get junior posts. It does not work out like that for English MPs who have a much poorer chance of getting into the Cabinet. The English are a very tolerant people, whatever we Welsh may say!

There used to be terrible bitterness between church and chapel during the campaign for disestablishment. I remember hearing the story of a meeting being addressed by the then Bishop of St Asaph who was attacking David Lloyd George. The chairman of the meeting introduced him with these words: 'David Lloyd George is the biggest liar in Wales, but thank God we have his match tonight – the Bishop of St Asaph.'

My own grandfather was a sturdy old Nonconformist. I often smile now when I think how he used to drop seeds in my mind. Grandparents are foolish to underestimate themselves. Here now in the autumn of my days I remember when I was a small child how he told me: 'George, never bend your back to a piece of wood or stone never mind what shape it is.' 'No Grandpa,' I innocently replied. I didn't realize what he was saying but he was actually telling me never to bow to a crucifix. Dear Grandpa, he was a product of a different age from ours! I thought of him every time I bowed to the Speaker's Chair in the House of Commons before I took my place, and I still think of him when I genuflect before the altar in an Anglican or Roman Catholic church. I have long since learned that respect for other people's way of worship is a matter of common courtesy.

There was an Anglican church in Tonypandy but it was not as well supported as the chapels. In fact I took a year off from the Central Hall and attended St Andrew's, Tonypandy, where I was confirmed when I was about eighteen. I used to get up early to go to Matins and be the only one there along with the vicar. St Andrew's was low church but High Church, with all its drama and changing of vestments during the service, seems to attract a very great many people. I have changed many of my early views. I like a church to look beautiful. I worship quite easily in a plain church without stained-glass windows or statues, but I confess I have grown more and more to like the sheer beauty of old cathedrals and the palpable atmosphere of churches in which people have worshipped for centuries. St David's Cathedral in Pembrokeshire has an atmosphere that makes me want to shout 'Hallelujah!' Llandaff has the same effect on me.

The pattern of worship is changing too. In the pre-war days it was the Sunday evening service that was packed; now it is the morning that is most popular as people want to keep the rest of the day free for their outings and television. In fact we may well become like America where in many states there is only the morning service of worship.

The Church in Wales has really stolen the clothes of the chapel. This began in the Depression when Anglican clergymen started to show a deeper interest in social and political issues. They also took a keen interest in the Welsh language when not so long ago none of them would have been Welsh speakers. At the Queen's Jubilee in 1977 when she came to the service in Llandaff Cathedral, the then Archbishop of Wales, an excellent man, preached in a mixture of Welsh and English, translating each sentence as he went.

The Church in Wales has become very radical, much more so than the Church of England used to be, but that too is changing. When two bishops were sworn in together recently, I heard somebody in the House of Lords say: 'Two more votes against the Government.' So the Chapel in which I grew up needs to recharge its batteries. In my judgement we need to put greater emphasis on prayer and on the straightforward preaching of the Gospel. This generation needs to realize the need for repentance if it is to know the glorious freedom enjoyed by those who are filled with the Holy Spirit. If the culture and strength of yesteryear is to flourish again in Wales the place to begin the restoration is in our religion.

CHAPTER THREE

OF PEOPLE
AND
PLACES

For a place as small as Wales the enormous part the country has played in British history is remarkable.

The people of Llantrisant, for example, are still proud of their connections with the Black Prince who was born on 15 July 1330 and who died in June 1376. The eldest son of Edward III, he was the first Duke of Cornwall, Prince of Wales, Prince of Aquitaine and Gascony and known only occasionally as Edward IV. The people of Llantrisant are still known as the Black Prince's men although strictly speaking this should only apply to the freemen of the town who wear a green and black striped tie for their ceremonies of Beating the Bounds every seven years and for the annual Court Leet meeting. The town's association with the Black Prince stems from the triumphant Battle of Crécy where an army of Llantrisant men, skilled in handling the longbow, fought alongside the Prince. For their help he awarded them the town charter and certain grazing rights. They have every right to be proud of their history, and the freemen have two silver maces which they display at their formal meetings and annual dinners. As a guest while Speaker of the House of Commons, I asked them the dates on their maces, knowing that the one in the Commons was dated CR2. Cromwell, you will remember, destroyed the original House of Commons mace, describing it as a 'bauble'. The Llantrisant men take great pride that their maces are stamped CR – Charles I. So Cromwell let some escape! Apparently the maces had been hidden in caves in the hills around the town. Partly because of its history and partly due to its commanding and easily defensible position, Llantrisant was for centuries far more important than Cardiff.

One of the town's more macabre claims to fame is the strange story of Dr Williams Price, who was still alive when my mother was growing up. She would often tell me the tale of this extraordinary man who wore a bizarre dress of green topped off with a fox fur on his head. Born near Caerphilly in 1800, he was a great eccentric and recluse who became a renowned surgeon, Chartist supporter and self-styled Druid. He believed in neither marriage nor Christianity and when he fathered a son by his housekeeper he called him Iesu Grist – Jesus Christ – presumably to offend the greatest number of people. The child died in infancy and on 18 January 1884, Dr Price took the body to the top of East Caerlan Hill on the edge of the old town and, placing it on top of a Hindu-style funeral pyre, set fire to it and then scattered the ashes on the mountain. There was a public outcry and Price was brought to trial for illegally disposing of the body. Despite public protests, he was acquitted and from then on cremation, although it had to be properly controlled, became legal. Dr Price, incidentally, went on to have a second son and a daughter.

Returning to memories of my own, I have a clear recollection of Keir Hardie, the founder of the Labour Party and the MP for Merthyr, coming to Tonypandy where he spoke from the top of a lorry in the old football ground we called the 'Mush'. As far as we were all concerned, Keir Hardie was very close to being a New Testament prophet. He was looked upon in that way and we were all very proud that it was Wales that gave him shelter when his native Scotland would not return him to Parliament. He was very Scottish and we used to like the story Keir Hardie told of when he was a boy working for a well-off baker who was, of course, a very religious man. Keir Hardie was a second or two late one day, and when he arrived at work he had to wait while the baker said grace, thanking God for all the bounty that was on their table. When the baker opened his eyes, he told Keir Hardie he was late and he was fired without his money. That story always outraged us radical chapel folk.

But it was not all politics and chapels in the valley and one of our true local heroes was my good friend Tommy Farr, who was born in Clydach Vale on 12 March 1914. His father was a 17-stone miner and bare-fist fighter who took on other local lads on the hills of Tonypandy. My earliest memories of Tommy are as the Tonypandy vinegar boy. He used to come into our street with his horse and cart shouting, 'Vinegar, vinegar'. On the back of the cart he had a cask with a little tap on it and people would take a jug to buy a pennyworth or more of vinegar. Tommy later became a miner for three years, but desperate to get out of the pits he too began fighting, becoming known as Kid Farr. He joined Joe Guess's boxing booth at the fairgrounds of South Wales. Among his early fights were those in 1929 at Ferndale against Kid Evans and at Tonypandy against Billy Jones. It was not until seven years later that he won the Welsh heavyweight title at Swansea against Jim Wilde. In the first six months of 1937 he went on to win the British Empire heavyweight title and Lonsdale Belt at Haringey against Ben Foord, to beat the handsome but boastful Max Baer of the United States of America over twelve rounds and to knock out Walter Neusel in the third round.

(above) *The unchanging face of Tonypandy . . . this row of houses in Gelli Street with its magnificent view over the Rhondda Fawr, has outwardly changed very little since the days when Tommy Farr used to sell vinegar from the back of a cart.*

(left) *Where it all began . . . Tydraw Street, Port Talbot, showing a typical face of Wales. This lady is, I think, pointing out the Methodist Chapel opposite my parents' house where I was born. Christened Thomas George Thomas there, I spent the first few years of my life, as a result of that choice of names, trying to avoid being unofficially rechristened 'Tommy Twice'!*

(above) *Friends and Neighbours One . . . making good use of the doorstep to practise the very Welsh art of conversation, this time in Ely Street where I lived for many years before moving to Cardiff as one of its MPs.*

(left) *Friends and Neighbours Two . . . a friendly face in Gelli Street, Tonypandy, where, rain permitting, the front door step still serves as a regular meeting place.*

(overleaf) *Modern times . . . perhaps an unnecessary use of the art of writing on a coach in Cardiff's dockland in the area once known as Tiger Bay, perhaps best remembered as the place that produced Shirley Bassey.*

But his greatest fight, which is still refought all over Wales, was on 30 August 1937 when he came within an ace of beating the great titleholder Joe Louis for the world heavyweight championship at Yankee Stadium, New York. He lost on a points decision over fifteen rounds. We all knew that fighting in America was different: lax rules, biased judges and referees, and partisan crowds. If he was to win we knew Tommy had to knock out Joe Louis, leaving no room for doubt. I remember that fight so well. It was one of the first to be broadcast live and I listened to it on our radio at about three in the morning. Those of us who had managed to listen to it were too excited to stay in and went out in the streets to talk about it. Both Tommy's eyes were cut in the fight; one eye had already been cut during training. The American crowd were impressed by his great showing in the face of ill-luck and by his enormous stamina. In the last round he drove Louis on to the ropes – a little more and Louis would have found himself out of the ring. 'If Farr could have produced that last desperate fling a few rounds earlier he would have given the all-night enthusiasts of Tonypandy something to cheer indeed,' wrote *The Times* boxing correspondent. There are many opinions voiced about the fight outcome, the crowd booing the decision in favour of Louis. But all were agreed on the wonderful clean-cut fighting and sportsmanship of the boxers. 'The contest was a credit to boxing,' said *The Times*. There was some consolation for Tommy. At a time when the average industrial wage in Britain was £3 a week, that one fight earned him £36,000. When Tommy Farr died in March 1985, his ashes were taken to be scattered on the hills of his beloved Tonypandy.

Wales has other great sportsmen too, many of whom I am proud to call my friends. There's Jack Peterson, another famous boxer. There's Tony Lewis, who went to school in Cowbridge and used to play cricket for Glamorgan, as unspoiled by success as a man could be. And of course Cliff Morgan, who was capped twenty-nine times by Wales as outside half from 1951 to 1958. His only boast is that the size of the twenty-ninth cap was the same size as the first one. And we all know that's true about him because they are all displayed at his old school in Tonyrefail.

Like so many valley boys who have gone on to be successful, Cliff Morgan never forgets his origins. He tells the story of his father who died while watching a televised international match in which Cliff was playing. Cliff had given his parents a colour

(above) *Private bus . . . a perfect piece of Art Deco preserved on a cottage restored by the National Trust in Merthyr Mawr, Mid-Glamorgan. The stained glass charabanc of the 1930s presumably marked the door of an owner-driver who ran his business from home.*

(right) *National bus . . . National Welsh to be precise, leaving the centre of Tonypandy.*

ELSH

*Skeleton staff . . . a
deserted Llantwit Major
beach presided over by a
little modern culture.*

television set and they were the only people in the streeet who had one, so the neighbours used to come in to watch it. One of those neighbours who was sympathizing with Cliff afterwards said, and he meant no harm by it, 'And what a pity he didn't live to see the end of the match.' Cliff, a Welsh speaker, has endless Welsh stories and comes from Trebanog, a tiny village three miles from Tonypandy. I used to tease him that it was an afterthought on the part of the Almighty, that He made Trebanog last, late on Saturday night before He took His rest on the Sabbath, but Cliff would have a riposte ready every time. He is the personification of the man every Welsh lad hopes to be.

Another great rugby man from the Rhondda is Cliff Jones whose father was a greengrocer in Tonypandy. Cliff also played as outside half for Wales, from 1934 to 1938 while a student at Cambridge and then Cardiff. He was president of the Welsh Rugby Union during the centenary year of 1980–81, and is now a Welsh selector, a trustee and life member of the Welsh Rugby Union. Like so many others who put a lot back into the game that has given them so much pleasure, he tours Wales lecturing around the schools to encourage the playing of rugby in particular.

As I reflect on my life now, I marvel at the rich variety of talent that has sprung from Wales and the good fortune that has allowed me to come to know so many of our most gifted folk. Three great friends from the entertainment world have been Geraint Evans, Harry Secombe and the late Stanley Baker, all of whom became knights.

To illustrate the smallness of Wales, Sir Geraint Evans and his fellow world-renowned singer called Stuart Burrows, and Merlyn Rees, who went on to become a Home Secretary in the Labour Government, all came from the same long row of old cottages in the Welsh mining village of Cilfynydd, two miles from Pontypridd. That just proves to me how much talent we waste, and not only in Wales. If those three boys from the same street could make it, depend on it there were plenty of others who could have had similar success. Tom Jones, another world-famous singer in a different mould, also hails from Treforest which is but two or three miles from Cilfynydd.

Geraint's great-grandmother was a pit doorgirl when she was eleven years old, opening the underground safety gates for the coal wagons to pass through on their journey from the face to the conveyor belts heading for the shaft. His father was a miner, and as a four-year-old during the General Strike, Geraint was a

Memories of better times . . . a 'high quality' fruiterer and fishmonger in a main street of Merthyr gives way to graffiti, the modern disease to disfigure all crumbling buildings.

78

FRUITERER .... AN & SON FISHMONGER 90

FOR QUALITY

RUBY C.C.F.C.
OK

(above) *The tug of royalty . . . the Welsh have been loyal to the Crown since the first Prince of Wales. Here, George VI gets his daily dose of letters at a wall box in Merthyr Mawr.*

(right) *A small piece of peace . . . a stile leads through to the fields by the sea at Llantwit Major, which saw the early Christian settlements set up in Wales.*

(overleaf) *A flight of history . . . this bird from the Maerdy Pigeon Club setting off on a training flight over the Rhondda, a quite rural valley before the boom time of coal, now returning to the tranquillity known by my grandfather when he migrated there in 1872.*

(left) *Keeping in touch One . . . this extraordinary public telephone box, probably dating back to the 1930s, has been let into a stone wall in Merthyr Mawr.*

(right) *Keeping in touch Two . . . everybody's friend, once the only contact with the larger world outside the smaller towns and villages, the postman at work in Llantwit Major.*

regular visitor to the soup kitchens and helped his uncles pick over waste at the pithead to find stray lumps of coal for the family fires. He was one of six Welshmen knighted in the 1969 Investiture honours, the first award to a singer still performing since 1907. His farewell concert in Wales was at Swansea in a marquee filled with 6000 people. It was very Welsh, very emotional. Sir Geraint was left in no doubt about the love all Wales has for him.

Stanley Baker, the outstandingly successful actor who died at a tragically early age, grew up in Ferndale, in the Rhondda Valley. I think we first met at a rugby match in Cardiff but I have always felt that, as two boys from the Rhondda, we belonged together – despite the difference in our ages. I have a particularly clear memory of him at Ninian Park, Cardiff, in 1964 when Harold Wilson came down to launch the General Election campaign in Wales. I was in the chair and Stanley was one of the speakers. He told this huge meeting how he had been born in Rhondda Fach, the son of a miner who had lost his leg in a pit accident, and went on to say how much his father and his background meant to him. Stanley told how when he was studying at home he used to go upstairs to his bedroom and sit on the window sill to use the light of the gas lamp outside to save his father's fuel bills. At ten o'clock his father would shout: 'Time to stop, Stanley,' and then go outside on his crutches to put out the lamp. Stanley didn't need the light any more and father was going to save that as well! Stanley's knighthood was announced in Harold Wilson's resignation honours list in May 1976, but sadly he died a month later in Spain, aged only forty-eight, before he received the accolade.

At the time of the Aberfan School disaster in October 1966, when I wanted to raise money for the people involved, I got in touch with Stanley Baker and with Harry Secombe, and wrote to Richard Burton, whom I had first met by chance during the war in the buffet on Cardiff station. Richard was extremely generous and sent us a very good cheque back. I took Harry to lunch in London to talk about what those in the entertainment world could do to help, for they were all going to give their services free and would raise a lot of money. When we were having lunch in the Travellers' Club, Pall Mall, I asked him if he had come by taxi and he said, no, he had come by car. I idly wondered where he had parked it, as I didn't want him to get a ticket. 'I didn't park it,' he said, 'I have a driver and he will be here after lunch.' We stood outside waiting for the car to come and I ignored the silver-grey

Buried treasure . . . a cockle gatherer at Pen-clawdd near Llanelli, displays a handful of his sand-smeared catch before it is washed and sent to market.

(overleaf) *Life goes on . . . as it has always done, on the sands at Pen-clawdd on the Gower where a cockle gatherer digs the beach in just the way his forefathers did for years before him.*

Rolls-Royce which glided to a stop outside the club. I kept on looking as Harry said: 'Here's my car.' When he saw the mixture of astonishment and admiration on my face, Harry gave one of his famous laughs and said, 'It goes with the job, George.'

I wish I could remember the names of all those who helped but I do know that I was very deeply moved by the way in which everybody responded. The news of Aberfan's coal tip sliding down the mountainside and smothering a school went to the four corners of the world, and touched everyone who heard the story. The idea of all those children being engulfed in a mountain of water and coal dust falling on them was too awful to contemplate without, however inadequately, attempting to make some amends.

I have been back once or twice to functions and have visited the swimming centre which was built with money given to the disaster fund. A new road has been built bypassing Aberfan, going straight up to Merthyr and making Aberfan even more isolated, with a motorway on the right and a motorway on the left, leaving the little valley village only to whose who live there.

Besides those who have crossed my path in later adult life, I remember too the boys in the class I taught in Marlborough Road School, Cardiff: boys like Dannie Abse, the brother of Leo who was for so many years my fellow Welsh Labour MP and a very cherished friend. Dannie went on to become a poet and a doctor. I remember him as the little boy who wore a blue serge suit with a waistcoat, always so neat. His mother was one of the most beautiful women I have ever met. I used to think that her very presence had a healing power for troubled people.

When I was teaching, every school day started with a compulsory half-hour scripture lesson and, along with every other teacher in the school, I would call out: 'Jews and Catholics leave now', and they had to stand outside the classroom until the lesson was over. It's embarrassing even to remember now, but at the time it did not apparently cause distress. Today, such a thing just could not happen.

While I had been at college in Southampton, I had become involved in some voluntary work with handicapped children and it was this experience that helped me in my last year of teaching to recognize that one of the boys in my class, as bright as a button but physically totally unco-ordinated, was in fact a spastic. That boy's experience was to be recalled for me in a strange way. Soon after I was elected to Parliament one of my greatest supporters told me her dark secret. She had a son, who never left the living-room except to be carried to bed. He was a spastic who could repeat everything that he heard on the radio. I was able to get the lad a peripatetic teacher who taught him to read and to write. He had three more years of life that were exciting for him because he could read voraciously. I decided that there must be other families with spastic children so I placed an advertisement in the *South Wales Echo* asking those seeking help with spastic children to come to a meeting in a hall I booked for the purpose. To my astonishment forty people turned up and as a result a Spastic Society was formed for Cardiff and District. That was like the planting of an acorn, for now the whole country is aware of the needs of spastics.

Among the happier memories were the Christmases in Ely Street. Every Christmas all the rest of the family would return, some to visit, some to stay. They were happy, noisy times. My sister Ada's husband, Will Webb, was a farm bailiff and incidentally a very good thatcher. Every Christmas Ada and Will would descend on Ely Street — three rooms downstairs, three rooms upstairs — with their troupe of six children. It would not have seemed like Christmas without them. I knew what I was in for when I went to Penygraig station to meet them. Ada was always loaded with carrots, potatoes, swedes, turnips; in fact we expected her to bring anything that grew in the ground. Sometimes she would bring a rabbit too as an extra feast. But we had to carry all these — and the younger children — home. The noise over Christmas was unbelievable, but so was the fun. One bed had to sleep four, two at the top, two at the bottom, with the resulting and frequent shout: 'Take your feet out of my face!' followed by roars of laughter. They were happy, innocent days!

CHAPTER FOUR

OF SLATE
AND
MOUNTAINS

To drive from Cardiff to North Wales is to enter another country. Indeed, for those Welshmen born in the south in the early part of this century, it might as well have been a foreign land. I have heard it said that it is only an invisible thread which links the north with the south of Wales. We in the valleys certainly said that the people of the north had spent all their money on the scenery.

A glance at a map gives no idea of the distance; in my young days a casual journey from Tonypandy to the north was really out of the question. Even today there are no motorways to this other country where the inhabitants cling fiercely to old customs and take delight in their Welsh language. As far as England was concerned, North Wales was discovered by the Victorian romantics who built the seaside hotels, housed their families for the summer in their own neo-Gothic creations and pushed through the railways which were to open up the area for holidaymakers from Cheshire, Liverpool and the Midlands. Then came the popular touring holidays of the 'thirties, tweed knickerbocker-clad men often spending more time beside their car than in it.

However it is explored, North Wales is a country of soaring mountains, miles of beaches, calm rivers and lakes, tortuous hairpin roads, friendly farms and guest houses. It is steeped in history too, with the Romans, Normans and the English princes all determined to conquer this isolated land. The English princes ringed the hills with great castle fortresses while along the Lleyn Peninsula, which points to Ireland, are dotted medieval churches, once places of pilgrimage in the Middle Ages.

Apart from this deep sense of history, North Wales is rich in little railways, nostalgic links with steam, which run on narrow gauges from Llanberis, Snowdon, Porthmadog and Tywyn. There are miniature railways at Rhyl and Colwyn Bay, and a funicular railway at Llandudno. You can even take the specially designed trains deep into the Llechwedd Slate Caverns and ride a train at Conwy Valley Railway Museum – wisely adults can only travel if they are accompanied by children. In the summer there are fun fairs and beach amusements too. The big fairs are at Rhyl and Pwllheli, puppet shows at Rhos-on-Sea, talent contests at Rhyl, Colwyn Bay and Llandudno or fossil hunting on the Great Orme. Many of the old crafts are carefully nurtured; in isolated villages you will come upon makers of wooden bowls, walking sticks, slate clocks, colourful Welsh weaves and the tradition of wrought-iron work, with smiths tapping away in ramshackle workshops.

The natural magnificence of North Wales is matched by the man-made splendour of Caernarfon. Nine miles from Bangor – the nearest railway station – and overlooking the Menai Straits where the River Seiont flows into the sea, Caernarfon is dominated by the castle, which looms up as you drive towards the centre. The thirteenth-century castle was commissioned by Edward I in 1283 to mark his victory over Llewelyn, last of the native Welsh princes. The castle, which took thirty-seven years to complete, became a focal point in the struggle between the English and Welsh for the rule of Wales. Caernarfon is a grey stone town with houses and shops all jostling for space. Outside the castle walls is an open air market with stalls of bric-à-brac, oranges, green wellingtons, anoraks and clothes pegs. From the castle environs a road runs down to the Slate Quay, now filled with small boats and yachts. Streets with engaging names like Hole in the Wall, Palace Street and Segontium Terrace turn off the Castle Square in which stands the statue of David Lloyd George who secured the survival of the castle in modern times. Although communications with the outside world are good, there is still an air of remoteness about Caernarfon.

The future Edward II was born as Edward of Caernarfon in the temporary residence alongside the site of the castle and was made Prince of Wales in 1301. Legend has it that the king presented his infant son to the Welsh leaders in fulfilment of a promise to give them a Prince who could speak no word of English. With the rise of the slate trade in the mid-nineteenth century, the population more than doubled. The building of Slate Quay spread the town along the River Seiont. The export of slate boosted shipping from here and the Harbour Offices built in 1840 indicate Caernarfon's importance as a nineteenth-century port, a role enhanced by the opening of Victoria Dock in the 1870s. The railway had arrived in 1852 to provide yet another outlet for slate. Cholera broke out in 1865 and this led to the development of the town on a more open plan, the basis for today's shape. Visitors still get the feel of a prosperous mid-Victorian town, which developed around the County Hall and gaol, built just outside the Castle walls.

Slate was as important to the north as coal was to the south. Slate from the enormous quarries in North Wales can be found on the roofs of houses not only all over Great Britain but throughout the world. Railways were built to link the quarries with the slate

One for the slate . . . in North Wales, slate is used for everything; no barbed wire, hedges or walls, the boundaries here are of good Welsh slate.

(overleaf) *Forgotten home . . . once ringing with the laughter of a family, this cottage lies rotting from neglect. Should we really turn away the English who have brought new life back to so many of our old homes?*

ports at Port Dinorwic, Port Penrhyn and Porthmadog. And as the miners had to fight for their rights and suffer in the process, so did the quarrymen whose ancestors had worked the slate for centuries. With the Industrial Revolution and the growth in housing, slate became a major industry, reaching its peak output in 1898. As the quarry owners began to grow rich, so the men felt they should be better protected and better rewarded. As in other major industries across Britain, demands began to be heard for the right to join a union.

The greatest hardship was at Bethesda in Gwynedd, where the quarry owner, Lord Penrhyn, opposed the formation of a union. Thousands of men were sacked for their beliefs and the lockout continued for three years from 1900 to 1903. During the lockout a people faced with starvation emigrated either to America or the South Wales mines. As with the miners in the south, they were starved back to work and the injustices of the owners were never forgotten. The seeds for reform had been well planted. The slate industry of North Wales was never to regain its importance but it was pressed into national service during the Second World War when major national treasures of art were hidden in the caves at Blaenau Ffestiniog. It is even rumoured that the crown jewels were kept safe in a similar way. One thing is for sure Blaenau, is a place for music, choirs, chapels and radical causes.

In my last year as Speaker I was asked to open the new station of the Ffestiniog Railway, once vital to the slate industry, but now mainly a scenic railway and very beautiful. What fascinated me was the enthusiasm of the people – solicitors, accountants, or maybe themselves manual workers from all walks of life – who had come from London and Manchester to work on the railway at weekends for nothing but the thrill. I treasure the gold medal they gave me which allows me to use the railway whenever I like.

It is extraordinary how steam has captured the imagination. There is a magic in it and I particularly remember standing once at dusk in the Vale of Glamorgan at a place called St George's just outside Cardiff where the train raced by and you could see the glow of the fire as the crew opened the fire door to throw on coal. The railways in and to Wales were, of course, all steam when I was first elected to Parliament in 1945 and one night I travelled on the footplate with the fireman and the driver on the night train from Cardiff via Gloucester to London. They allowed me to throw some of the coal on to the fire. It was a heavy job and I

wasn't very good at it so they let me stand and watch for red lights. I missed them, of course, as we were going so fast.

Along with steam, slate fell victim to progress and by the 1960s most of the major quarries had closed and their dilapidated buildings and rotting ironwork amongst tons of waste slate and abandoned steam locomotives mark the countryside like giants' graveyards. The five still working now depend heavily on tourism but you can still get the thrill of watching a true craftsman at work. These men had a skill which must never be lost. They can take a piece of slate and using the chisel and hammer get a fine, thin piece that could go straight on to a roof. The rest of us could try for a month and still break it. There is no easy way to master a hereditary skill that has been passed down the generations from father to son. As Secretary of State for Wales, I visited Llechwedd, one of the largest quarries.

Years later, when I was Speaker, I went to the Niagara Falls and unveiled a slate slab from Llechwedd to commemorate the golden jubilee of the Singing Festival of the Welsh in America. It was in 1979 – and I remember it so well for it was in the week that Lord Mountbatten had been murdered by the IRA while he was on holiday at his home in County Cork. After the unveiling ceremony we sang ourselves nearly unconscious, hymns following one after the other for hours and hours; we would have a break for a meal and then go back to the singing festival.

On the Saturday night there was a banquet for fifteen hundred people for which the mayor, whose family had come from Ireland, arrived late. Sitting next to his wife, I had Mountbatten's death very much on my mind. I was flying back overnight to go to the funeral in Westminster Abbey to represent the House of Commons. So after greeting the mayoress I naturally said: 'Isn't the news terrible about the murder of Lord Mountbatten?' To my surprise she replied: 'There's another side to that.' And I could only say that there was never another side to murder: murder was murder. She went on to say that she had three relatives in Long Kesh prison in Ulster. By now I was very angry and told her they were almost certainly there for either murder or attempted murder. I don't think she knew too much about them and said only that she believed in a united Ireland. I told her that I believed that Texas belonged to Mexico but that it was not my business. At this point our voices were getting higher and people began to look at us, so the subject was dropped.

Wizened age . . . a tree that has withstood years of battering from the elements, rather like the Welsh themselves!

(overleaf) *Steps in time . . . the old steps that lead down to Blaenau Ffestiniog, once home of one of the most successful slate quarries in North Wales, now sadly making money only from tourists.*

99

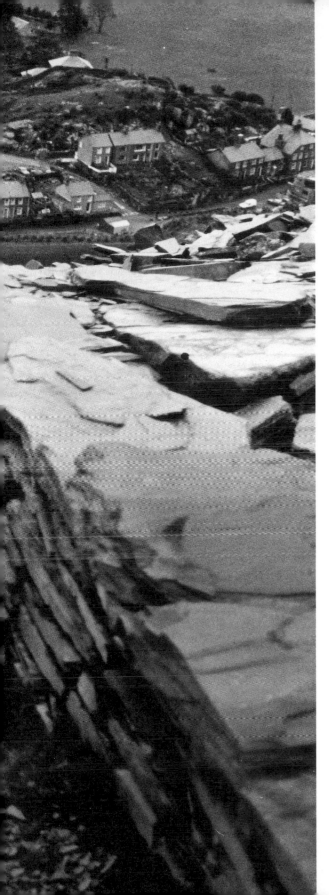

At the end of the evening we all sang 'Land Of My Fathers' – some sang it in Welsh – then 'Oh America', with hand on heart, and finally 'Oh Canada' as the Canadian Welsh had joined us. This was to be the end but I jumped up and seized the microphone and said: 'Dear friends, I am from the Mother Country – God Save The Queen.' They all stood up and sang 'God Save The Queen' – even the mayor and his wife who had been saying the most terrible things to me.

Thankfully the cause of nationalism in Wales has never reached the pitch to be found in Ireland, although for a time in the late sixties the bombs did begin to explode in Wales. People seem to forget it now. But fifty bombs went off in Wales in the months leading up to the investiture of Prince Charles. On one occasion I flew to Pembrey Sands to visit an airman injured by a bomb blast – poor boy, he was only there doing his duty to protect the country. It turned out that he and his wife were both Methodists and they recognized me at once through Methodism, not as a politician. The luckiest escape came when the Welsh Office in Cardiff was blown up; a policeman had walked by only a minute before and he had only gone down the end of the road when the place went up. Can there ever be justification for this kind of violence?

As the explosions continued through 1968 and the first part of 1969, there was genuine cause for concern for the safety of Prince Charles as the time for his investiture drew near. David Lloyd George, who won a by-election to become Liberal Member for Caernarfon Boroughs when he was only twenty-seven, always capitalized on the town's historical significance. He held the seat for fifty-five years during which time he became Chancellor of the Exchequer and Prime Minister from 1916 to 1922. It was he who persuaded King George V to hold the investiture of the Prince of Wales in its supposedly original place. In 1911, at a cost of two million pounds in today's figures, the ceremony was held with both castle and town benefiting from necessary repairs.

This was all very much in my mind when, as Secretary of State for Wales, I was responsible with the Earl Marshal of England, the Duke of Norfolk, for organizing the investiture of Prince Charles as Prince of Wales at Caernarfon in 1969. We had a budget of £200,000, much to the unhappiness of the Duke who was continually referring to his father's notes detailing the organization of the 1911 investiture which was altogether a much grander affair. David Lloyd George always had an eye to business and had persuaded the people of Caernarfon that the investiture would be good for them. He had persuaded them too that he was the voice of Welsh nationalism, a role he soon abandoned when he entered national politics, along with his many promises, particularly the pledge that Wales would have her own parliament.

That whole business of a parliament for Wales is now dead, although some sections of the Labour Party are again talking about an Assembly, despite the fact that Neil Kinnock was one of the very strongest opponents of the original devolution proposals, even turning down a post in the Government. Ironically it was the anti-devolution campaign led by him and Leo Abse that first brought him real public attention. Tempers ran very high and it still seems strange to me, looking back, that Lloyd George did not have to face the hostility that was so evident in the 1960s and that seemed an inevitable adjunct to modern nationalist movements.

I was very aware of this latent hostility when it was suggested that Prince Charles should spend a term at Aberystwyth, the University College of Wales, before the investiture. I thought it was not only rather patronizing to Wales but unnecessarily provocative. There was a particularly nationalist flavour at Aberystwyth, the first Welsh University College – the mother college – founded on the pennies of the workers. There is a special pride in Wales that it was the miners and railway workers who collected to start a college there so that we should have a place to give an opportunity to Welsh boys to graduate and take their place in the world. The university's original Gothic-style building, a rather splendid piece of architecture, is still used but the main campus is just outside the town, a seaside resort especially popular with people from the north of England.

As in many other holiday towns the Victorians have left their mark – the cliff railway on Constitution Hill is still a tourist must. The Victorians built the six-compartment train as a 'conveyance for gentlefolk' to save them tramping the 430 feet from the beach to the top of the cliff. There was also the inevitable long pier, which equally inevitably has become considerably shorter over the years. I can only guess what the Victorians would make of the Chinese restaurant, bingo hall and ice-cream parlour that now grace the pier. Their successors on the town council carried out their own improvements to cope with the boom times but sadly

The majesty of the North . . . a stream, swollen by the autumn rains, tumbles down a mountainside that protects the North, not just from the English but the South Welsh as well!

these have not survived so well. The pink-painted King's Hall built for dances still stands, but hardly proudly, as does the public shelter built in 1924 to protect holidaymakers from the rain – weather has always been the enemy of the British seaside resort.

Today, the town's seaside pleasures are the North Shore, an attractive and safe place for children, and South Beach near the harbour. The cliff railway remains popular and on top of the cliff station is the world's biggest Camera Obscura from which you can see the span of Aberystwyth in great detail. There have been complaints from local residents, fearing their privacy! The Vale of Rheidol Railway – British Rail's only narrow gauge steam-operated railway – takes visitors up the wooded valley to Devil's Bridge for the spectacular falls. Prettily washed hotels, guest houses and halls of residence line Marine Terrace on North Shore, a picture seen on many postcards.

Apart from the university, serious visitors to the town can find the written history of Wales in a collection of rare manuscripts at the National Library of Wales at Penglais. And it was this side of Aberystwyth, where nationalism seems part of the very air, rather than the ice creams and donkey rides, that had its influence on Prince Charles, an influence that would have been significantly different had he gone to one of the other six colleges that make up the University of Wales. Swansea or Cardiff, for example, would I believe have given him a more rounded picture of what I see as the real Wales, a place proud of its heritage and independence but nevertheless firmly a part of the United Kingdom. Once the decision was taken for Prince Charles to go to Aberystwyth I supported it publicly despite some serious misgivings. The Prince took rooms with his equerry and private detective in the Pantycelin hostel, named after the great hymn writer. He was young and impressionable, loose from all the royal restraints and with Welsh nationalists all around him.

One of his main tasks while at the university was to learn the Welsh language, and he was given a tutor who was a well-known Welsh Nationalist. He must have been a good teacher and Prince Charles a good pupil because he made an excellent speech in Welsh at the investiture. He likes to tell me that his Welsh is better than mine – and there are times when it is! He certainly seemed to be influenced by the thinking at Aberystwyth, and when he made a speech in Cardiff that year, on being given the freedom of the city, it was not unsympathetic to nationalism. Prince Charles must have found it all very different from Cambridge, but despite my misgivings at the time his term at Aberystwyth will have been useful to him. And I'm sure, looking back, that he was never in any physical danger, although at the time we were all very concerned for his safety and fairly elaborate plans were laid to protect him. Just before he was due to arrive at the university, several police officers were moved on to the campus, disguised – as we thought – as gardeners. It was foolish really as all the students realized at once who they were!

I still remember the investiture clearly, not just the bombs and the personal antagonism towards me from the nationalists, but for the obvious pleasure the ceremony gave to the Queen, for the beauty of the surroundings, which owed much to Lord Snowdon as Constable of the castle, and for the fact that it marked the real beginning of public duty for Prince Charles, who secured a special place in Wales' affection.

During the run up to the investiture I would occasionally escape to Beaumaris, a beautiful, peaceful town on the Anglesey side of the Menai Straits. The Norman invaders called it Beau Maris – Lovely Flatland; from the dark blue waters between the wooded beaches of Anglesey and the mainland can be seen the spectacular mountains of Snowdonia. Standing guard over it all is Beaumaris Castle, one of the fortresses begun by Edward I in 1295. There is a fifteenth-century early Tudor house in the main street, an old gaol built in 1829 in Steeple Lane which has in its yard a wooden treadmill, one of the last to be used in Britain, and high on one of the outside walls is the door from which condemned men stepped out to be executed. Facing Anglesey across the Menai Straits is the university and holiday city of Bangor, gateway to Anglesey and the Ogwen Valley, and dominated by the cathedral in the lower, busy area of the city which, with shops and houses crowded together, is almost medieval.

As Secretary of State for Wales, I was often accompanied by my Permanent Secretary, Sir Goronwy Daniel, when we went to the north, usually to be attacked for failing to do enough to improve employment in the region. Often I would point to a house way up on the mountain and say: 'What a lonely place for a child to grow up.' Yet so many professors and geniuses have come from those little places right up on the hills, as though as youngsters they had nothing to do but to study or be gripped by the urge to get on.

Some cousins of Dad Tom lived in a place called Dinas Mawddwy, east of Dolgellau, and I used to visit them in their farmhouse on the hill. We used to sit right in alongside the open fire under a sort of arch. It was great hospitality, with simple food and plenty of it, though primitive – no bathroom or anything – but they could hold forth about poetry. It is always wrong to view people who come from a small isolated place as less cultured than those from big cities with plenty of facilities. Often the very lack of facilities means they are much better read.

Maybe television and tourism are changing the old ways and many of the changes are inevitable and necessary. Tourism particularly is vital to provide much needed income and work for the north, but there appears now to be an understanding that we should try to preserve the best of the old. In that we are helped by the builders of the past, for even as holiday developments spring up around the ancient towns, they are not able to diminish the splendour of the countryside nor the magnificence of the castles, castles like Harlech, yet another monument to Edward I and the last to hold out for Charles I, surrendering in 1647. Or like Conwy, standing at the mouth of the Afon Conwy. The town shelters under walls by the river bank where two bridges span the river: Telford's 1826 suspension bridge and Robert Stephenson's tubular bridge which was effectively a rehearsal for the much larger structure over the Menai Straits. The first train passed over the Conwy Bridge in 1848; the Britannia Bridge opened in 1850. On the quay is a house said to be the smallest in Britain and furnished as a mid-Victorian Welsh cottage, but Conwy still stands much as it did when Edward I was besieged in his own fortress by the Welsh and had to be saved by the provident arrival of an English ship. To travel through the north of the country is truly to revisit our history.

CHAPTER FIVE

OF POLITICS
AND
POWER

The day that really changed my life and that finally led to the Speaker's chair in the House of Commons some thirty years later was that day in July 1945 when I was elected Labour MP for Cardiff Central with a majority of 4524. Jim Callaghan was elected in Cardiff South.

When my stepfather died in 1948, Mam and I decided there was not much point in my having to travel the extra twenty miles from Cardiff each time I came home, so we left our house in Ely Street, Tonypandy, and moved to a flat in the constituency. It was a terrible wrench, and even though Mam had made up her mind that she would not follow the Welsh custom and burst into tears as we left, the sight of the weeping neighbours all gathered round was too much for her, and she did cry when we got into the car. It seems strange now with the age of the motorway and the modern motor car, but for a long time we were terribly homesick, even though we were only twenty miles away.

I soon realized that it was a big mistake for any Member to live in his constituency. Ignorant or disturbed people put terrible things through the letter box, and the doorbell would ring at any hour. When I was away, Mam would come down to answer it, usually to be met with indignation because I wasn't there. One freezing night when I was home, two young men who were sleeping rough appeared on the doorstep. They were dirty, unkempt, and complete strangers to me. Pointing to his companion, one of them said: 'George, he's ill.' I invited them in and we struggled to get the sick man up the seventeen stairs to our flat. We had no spare accommodation so I rang the Social Services and explained I had someone with me who normally slept rough and was obviously very ill. I asked the duty officer to arrange shelter for the night in accordance with statutory provisions.

He refused and we had high words, his attitude being that he could do nothing as it was so late at night. I then rang the police, so often maligned these days for being uncaring, who told me that they would give him shelter for the night. I made quite sure the sick man would not be prosecuted for vagrancy, and, with difficulty, we took him back down the stairs and into my car. The other man disappeared into the night, and I drove to the police station. They assured me they would give him a bed and a cup of tea, and I promised to take him to hospital in the morning. When I rang at eight that morning he was dead.

It was yet another lesson: to be patient if people come in need of help. I have always been thankful that I took him to the police station, and that he was cared for. I could not do much, but at least I could look myself in the face. It would have been too late after he had died to wish that I had done something.

We left that flat within three years. Mam never took to it, and when she was seventy she had a heart attack. The doctor told me: 'If you want to keep your mother, you will have to move to the ground floor,' and so we bought our bungalow in King George V Drive East, Cardiff.

Once I was an MP I set about tackling the problem of the many thousands of people who had only the leasehold of their homes. When I became a candidate, the first thing I did was to pinpoint the ten major headaches for the people in Cardiff Central. Apart from the transient problem of bringing our men home in a fair way at the end of the war, I soon discovered that at every meeting I addressed, somebody would raise the question of leasehold. Throughout Wales particularly, there were many leasehold properties which were then coming to the end of the agreement. Not only would the people who had lived in those places for so long lose their homes, they were also expected to pay the most unreasonable repair and decoration bills before they handed them back to the freeholder.

Typical of the problem were two sisters who lived in the house left to them by their parents. Now in their old age they would not only be evicted from their home but they faced a bill for £400, which in the 1940s was a large amount of money, to put the house into a proper state of repair before the ground landlord would accept it back. It was a matter that transcended party politics, although when I asked the Welsh Parliamentary Party, which consisted of all the Parties in the House, to have a national petition in Wales they refused – so I organized my own.

During the course of my campaign, which lasted twenty years before the Labour Government of Harold Wilson passed the Leasehold Reform Act, I made a speech in the House of Commons attacking one of the biggest ground landlords in Cardiff. One of their directors was the Conservative MP Sir John Foster QC, a delightful fellow who became my target: 'The Honourable and Learned gentleman opposite comes down to Cardiff with a great big bag to collect the rent – that is the limit of his interest in Cardiff because having got the rents he disappears back to London.' He was so indignant. Of course he did not bring a bag to

(above) *Quenching a thirst . . . the Taff Vale Brewery at Merthyr which was built in 1904 just two years before I was born. The valleys were thirsty then!*

(left) *Yesterday's culture . . . today's decay. The cinema in Tonypandy where I used to laugh at Charlie Chaplin and had those first flickering glimpses of the world outside.*

collect the rents, but he was defending the system and therefore vulnerable to attack. He challenged me to repeat my accusation outside the house, presumably with a view to suing me for slander, as I would not be protected by the privilege of the House of Commons.

I let it be known that I would be repeating my charge at a meeting in Cardiff, the following Sunday, after chapel. We would never think of holding a meeting that conflicted with chapel hours. After chapel was acceptable – I used to argue that it was a continuation of the Lord's work. Meetings are seldom held on Sundays now, but for reasons not connected with respect for the Sabbath. That particular Sunday meeting had attracted considerable publicity following Sir John's challenge and was well attended. I told the meeting I was going to read them an extract from Hansard, the official record of the proceedings of the House of Commons, that contained my original attack. I said: 'I would

like to know if it is now an offence in this country to read Hansard to the people.' I heard no more from Sir John. He was a man for whom I had a very high personal regard. It was the system that really aroused my fury.

On that particular occasion the attack was on a Member of Parliament who was identified with a system many people believed should be changed, but it is also true that it usually pays to take on the big names in the House of Commons. Nye Bevan, for example, used to go for Churchill; he didn't bother about the little folk who were not known in the country. If you could provoke the great name to attack you, the story would probably be reported in the newspapers and you would also get known.

I was helped, for example, in 1964 when Henry Brooke, then the Conservative Home Secretary, came to Cardiff in the General Election campaign and launched a personal attack on me for my views on leasehold. That did me no harm at all. Looking back on the leasehold campaign I can understand the objections from the Tories, but I am at a loss to explain why there was so much reluctance to denounce it from some sections of the Labour Party. We really had a chance to go to town because we were the champions for a property-owning democracy, which until then had been the slogan of the other side. In a sense we were stealing their clothes, but they had never seen fit to take their slogan further and give people the right to buy the freehold of a house they had lived in most, if not all, of their life.

It was a keynote campaign and certainly gained me vital support in the 1959 General Election when Labour generally had a very tough time. It was in the 'You have never had it so good' days of Harold Macmillan. I remember walking down the steps of Cardiff City Hall after the announcement of the results and telling Jim Callaghan that I felt naked with a majority of only 3000. He replied: 'That is riches compared to mine.' For at that election his majority had slipped to 868.

The results shook us because they showed us to be completely out of touch with the feeling of the people; we had thought we were going to do better. I did, however, have doubts on polling day. I was walking near Llandaff Cathedral and said good morning to two old ladies. I had just been into the Cathedral so was not wearing my rosette as I always took it off if I was anywhere near a place of worship. One of the ladies recognized me just the same. She turned to the other and said: 'This is the

Olde worlde charm . . . the bed and breakfast trade is booming in Wales, even if this establishment does seem rather selective.

*One for the road . . .
Vaynor Quarry near Cefn
lies silent in the morning
before work starts on
quarrying roadstone for
use in road building across
the country.*

(overleaf left) *Scenes familiar
. . . the more things change
in the valleys, the more
they appear to stay the
same, as shown in this
timeless piece of Merthyr.*

(overleaf right) *The bravest
man in the Rhondda . . .
here at the Maerdy – or is
it Mardy? – Workingmen's
Conservative Club is the
source of the Rhondda's
oldest joke: club
membership about 160,
Conservative voters about
10.*

gentleman who is trying to get dear Mr Macmillan out.' I said: 'No! No! You are making a mistake, I'm the person trying to get George Thomas in!'

Even before I was elected an MP, I had a deep regard and love for Cardiff, having taught in the city before and during the war when I had lost many friends and seen the school where I was working destroyed. Indeed, it was on the day after the school had been bombed that I had an early brush with what I saw as unthinking officialdom.

The school inspector, a blustering fellow, met all the staff to announce: 'Well, the school is finished.' I was the spokesman, although I was twenty years younger than everyone else, and I said, 'This school is not finished, sir, the building is – the school is still intact.' And that is how I feel about many parts of Wales where there have been physical changes. The buildings are finished but the community is not.

The underlying affection I had for Cardiff was to grow during the nearly forty years I represented its people. It is indeed a rich and marvellous place, and certainly it has its rough spots. The singer Shirley Bassey came from one of the toughest, which was then known as 'Tiger Bay', down in the docks. That name was dropped from use years ago when the citizens living there took strong exception to the label put upon them.

Before the war Cardiff had the largest coloured population of any city in Britain, but most of them stayed in the self-imposed ghetto of dockland where the policemen always walked in twos. The people themselves rarely came over Bute Bridge into town. I remember after the war when they began to want jobs in the shops in the centre of Cardiff and many places did not want to have black girls as assistants. It was very hard for them and that was the first time I became conscious of the denial of rights for black people.

Some of the older people still talk of the trouble early in the century when a number of different nationalities arrived at the then-thriving docks. Among them came the Chinese who were great gamblers and were accused by the local people of setting up opium dens in their settlements in the docks. There was a great deal of antagonism at the time and the police often had to intervene in disputes between the two communities, but relations have since been repaired and in 1982 Cardiff was twinned with the Chinese town of Xiamen. There have been various cultural exchanges and Welsh architects have even drawn up plans to build a mini-Cardiff to be used as a leisure centre over there.

The other main immigrants to Wales, along with the English, the black groups and the Chinese, were the Irish who came over to work in the steel works. To this day there is a very large proportion of people with Irish origins in Merthyr Tydfil and Cardiff. St Patrick's Day is celebrated in those towns with as much fervour as St David's Day. The Irish, who seem to have a flair for heavy work, naturally brought their religion with them and so the Roman Catholic Church grew in power in South Wales. It has to be said too that the Irish, with their long memories of British rule in Ireland, were a great help to the Labour movement in Wales.

The most significant individual immigrants to Cardiff, however, must be the Bute family who first arrived from Scotland in 1766 and made their home in Cardiff Castle. Originally a Roman fort – remains of the walls are still to be found – the Normans raised a large mound in the centre of the site and built a wooden stockade and keep on top. By the end of the twelfth century this had been replaced in stone in order to withstand repeated Welsh attacks. I remember telling one class how the elder son of William the Conqueror had been held in the castle for 'nineteen long winters'. One cheeky little fellow said: 'You said long winters sir – were they short summers?' I could only say that the winter always seemed longer.

The grounds of the castle as it stands today are largely the work of Lancelot Brown, better known as Capability Brown, who designed the gardens in 1776. The present castle was restored in the nineteenth century by William Burges. Depending on your point of view Cardiff Castle is either a masterpiece of Victorian art or a monument to bad taste. Those of us who live in Cardiff are very proud of our Castle and its long history. Over the years, the Butes carried out most of the development of Cardiff, including large parts of the docks and much of the housing estates. Their stake in the city was colossal. In the middle 1930s the family sold virtually half of Cardiff for £20 million. Had they held on for a few more years, they would have got that for one building.

As the Butes were beginning to sell in Cardiff, other developers were carrying on building in the city. One estate near the General railway station by the River Taff – that's why we are called 'Taffies' – was dubbed 'Temperance Town', as the builder refused to allow any public houses to open there.

Too much drink was a problem then as it is now, and for some years before the war I had been Secretary of the Workers Temperance League in Wales. I had been deeply impressed by Dr Salter, the Labour MP for Bermondsey, who claimed that two per cent of all those who drank alcohol would, for some reason in their make-up, inevitably become alcoholics. The trouble is that we can never tell who the two per cent are until it is too late! The dangers of drinking are all too obvious, as I know from my own father's experience and my mother's suffering. Once someone is enmeshed in the alcohol trap it is difficult for them to escape.

There are many examples but one that sticks in my mind is the highly qualified mate on the ship that took me from Middlesbrough to Halifax, Nova Scotia, in the 1950s. He became drunk and incapable in Canada and repeated the performance when we arrived back in Liverpool. I next saw him in Cardiff as a car park attendant when I was on my way to visit Cardiff Castle.

It was in the 1950s that the then Marquis of Bute gave Cardiff Castle to the city with the provision that there was always to be a room there where he could stay if he wished. It was the hope of a great many of us that Prince Charles would make it his home, but knowing the castle myself and how cold it can be I don't blame him for staying away!

Of all the grand buildings connected with the city, I have a particular love of Llandaff Cathedral, the site of an early Christian monastery founded at a time when Saxon England was still heathen. Little is known about the early history of Llandaff but it is believed that the Cathedral, which dominated the town, was founded about 530 by St Teilo who had come there from western Wales. It was my great good fortune that the Cathedral was in my constituency and as a result my seat was always right under the magnificent Epstein statue of Christ in Majesty, which was supported on concrete plinths straddling the nave, looking rather like the pillars of a modern motorway. The Cathedral was hit by a bomb during the war and the statue was put there as part of the restoration work. Initially, and I suppose inevitably, it caused controversy. Now, however, it has become one of the main attractions.

People rushing into the Cathedral may miss one of the more unusual pieces of artwork adorning a cathedral anywhere. The wall facing the road is decorated with the crowned heads of the kings of England. Edward VIII is there – but without the crown!

In camouflage, a derelict quarryman's house hides in the slate of Penrhyn.

(overleaf) The power of slate . . . Gloddfa Ganol, once at the heart of the slate industry, now open to the public as a tourist attraction.

(above) *Past glories . . . the quarries at Penrhyn once as important to the North as coal was to the South.*

(left) *Ivy League . . . a slate wall and steps at Blaenau Ffestiniog.*

(overleaf *A losing battle . . . trees at Penrhyn Quarries fight for a foothold in a torrent of discarded slate.*

(above) *So prim and proper . . . a cemetery with a freshly dug grave at Llangwynnadl.*

(left) *Still coal-fired . . . the homes at Blaenau Ffestiniog, now best known for its railway.*

(overleaf) *Overview . . . Blaenau Ffestiniog as seen from the old quarry at Gloddfa Ganol.*

Autumn leaves . . . Snowdonia, to the south east of Snowdon, prepares for the winter.

CHAPTER SIX

OF SEA
AND
STATE

The M4 motorway has really opened up South Wales to the traveller from England, now welcomed by most of us unlike our ancestors who did their best to keep the English away. Once over the border – not quite so exciting as perhaps it should be unless you are a Welshman coming home – you realize how lucky the people of South Wales are. They can easily escape to the glories of the Brecon Beacons National Park, grassy mountains, little fields, tucked away villages and mountain roads which look down on the valley towns of Merthyr, Tonypandy and Rhymney, names in the history of coal and iron that reach deep into every Welshman's soul. There are the endless beaches too of Dyfed and Gower, the Pembrokeshire Coast National Park and the resorts of Tenby, Barry Island and Porthcawl, with the great cosmopolitan cities of Swansea and Cardiff.

The Welsh might not like to hear me say it but there are even some parts of the country that resemble England, particularly the Vale of Glamorgan and Llantwit Major. My brother Ivor and I came to know it so well before the war when we took Mam out for drives to try to restore the use of her legs after our doctors had said she would never walk again. She did, largely I'm sure because of the gentle walks the three of us took around Llantwit Major.

Ivor and I bought a Morris 8 on hire purchase and used to drive out from Tonypandy through to Cowbridge, the centre of the Vale of Glamorgan's farming community, just 12 miles west of Cardiff. Known as the capital of the vale, its wide main street, fine inns and homely shops would make it an ideal setting for a period television series. Now just two ruined towers remain of the original city walls, but you can still feel the history of Cowbridge as you walk through the streets. Inside the Church of the Holy Rood is a memorial to Dr Benjamin Heath Malkin, whose descriptions of South Wales became the regular guidebooks for early nineteenth-century travellers to the area.

The eighteenth-century stonemason and collector of manuscripts, Edward Williams, was another famous son. Williams, known in Wales by his Bardic title, Iolo Morgannwg, recreated the now familiar Gorsedd of Bards associated with the National Eisteddfod of Wales and is buried nearby at Flemingston. Thomas Carlyle was a frequent visitor to the vale, and articles in *The Times* by his friend here, John Sterling, were eagerly read by local people who looked out for the stage-coach carrying the paper as it rumbled into Cowbridge.

My sister Dolly lived in Cowbridge in the 1920s, just opposite the road that branches off to Llantwit Major. Now there are lovely modern houses built where her cottage was, but when Dolly lived there, her toilet was across the road. Nowadays it would be an impossible task of course: you could wait half an hour before the traffic would allow you to cross the road. My first memories of Cowbridge are of the early days of the motor car when we all thought they were a terrible menace, even though we would only see one every ten minutes or so.

There is a pastoral feel to the roads through the vale to Llantwit Major and it is sometimes hard to remember that the industrially scarred Rhondda is so near to this so very tranquil place. Llantwit, an ancient town, is built out of sight of the sea at the head of the Colhugh Valley. We used to like Llantwit Major where the old people often recounted the story of how St Paul had visited the town. Now I know there is not a shred of evidence anywhere to support it, but because we liked the idea we were willing to accept it. Llantwit Major is certainly an old monastic centre, and during the period of the Celtic church before the Conquest it was a centre of Christian teaching. Both St David and St Teilo are believed to have studied in its Christian monastery of which there is now no trace, so I am not a bit surprised that the people should believe that St Paul was there too. Who knows, one day someone might find that he wrote a letter to them – now that would be something for the New Testament!

Mam, Ivor and I used to drive along the coast to watch the waves and walk on the beach – there never was a place like Llantwit Major for so many crabs underneath the rocks. It's a very rocky beach, and when you lifted up a stone you would invariably find crabs. I was very brave with the smaller ones but I must say when I once came across a fair-sized one – and I knew it could give you a nasty bite – I decided to let him go. I wasn't looking for food, only for the excitement of catching them.

It is an unspoiled part of the Welsh coast, typical of our most beautiful scenery. Tourism is changing attitudes now but I don't think the rest of the United Kingdom realizes just how beautiful South Wales is. From Llantwit Major we drove along the narrow coastal road past St Donats Castle that is now the home of the Atlantic College. I have since visited it from time to time and it is undoubtedly an excellent place, with its own sea rescue service recognized by the RNLI.

Atlantic College was founded in 1962 by Dr Kurt Hahn, famous first for Salem and then Gordonstoun, and Air Marshal Sir Lawrence Darvall. They were particularly concerned for young people aged 16–19, and placed the emphasis on high academic achievements, rugged outdoor pursuits and better international understanding. Prince Charles is President of the International Council of United World Colleges, of which Atlantic College was the first of six formed to promote international understanding. There are 368 students from 60 countries at St Donats where fees are over £5000 a year, although it is college policy to open places to all.

High academic and personal qualities are the entry considerations. The syllabus is that of the International Baccalaureate and its peace studies course is one of the few in Britain. Lord Mountbatten was patron and president of the International Council of United World Colleges from 1969 until his death, and his place as patron has been taken by the Queen. Prince Charles was criticized after he had made a speech in America to raise money for the colleges in which he spoke of the need for an élite. I know from my visits to St Donats what a marvellous opportunity it gives to young people from all over the world. Of course it is élitist, but I agree very much with Prince Charles. After all, there is room for élitism in every society – if we want life to be monochrome, all on one level, it wouldn't be very interesting or exciting, would it?

Our weekend trips with Mam would take us on to Southerndown and Dunraven Bay where the Victorian houses perched on the edge of the cliffs overlooking the Bristol Channel give an idea of the peaceful charm and leisured lifestyle of the early nineteenth century. Right up to the First World War notices near the lodge at Dunraven Bay proclaimed: 'Mixed Bathing Strictly Prohibited' and 'Ladies are requested to bathe on the East Side of the Bay and Gentlemen on the West Side'. How things have changed! You could also buy refreshments in a tent in what is now the car park. Later the business was transferred to Ogmore-by-Sea and taken over by a Mr Dixon who owned a donkey named Harkaway. Attached to a car, the donkey would transport laundry baskets to and from the Southerndown Road station for hotels and houses in the area. Mr Dixon was never known to beat Harkaway; indeed he made the journey easier for him by brushing the roadway with a broom!

Dunraven Castle has now been demolished, yet for most of the villagers in the area it was once a main source of employment. The Seamouth Café was originally the Dunraven Castle laundry where laundry maids used huge wooden mangles, the rollers being filled with heavy stones or pebbles and winched by chains across the clothes. The late Queen Mary, when Princess of Teck before her marriage, stayed at the castle. One day her mother the Duchess got her stockings wet while paddling in the sea, so she borrowed some from Jenny David, a farmer's wife and ate Jenny's Welsh cakes as her stockings dried out.

Our weekend drives would end at Ogmore-by-Sea where we would usually have a cup of tea before turning round and driving home. Before the First World War, this part was known as Sutton, taking its name from the Sutton stone quarries. Such is the beauty of this coastline that on 16 June 1972 a plaque was unveiled to mark it as a place of outstanding beauty. This was the third such plaque erected in Wales, the other two being on the Rhigos Mountain and on Llantrisant Common. They are the work of the Evangelical Sisterhood of Mary as a reminder of God's gift of natural beauty. Like most things modern in Wales, the plaque, set in a block of Sutton Stone, is bilingual.

From a fold in the limestone downs of Ogmore the road enters St Brides Major through an entrance framed by a grove of trees. Until cars made the journey to St Brides so much easier, it seems to have been a forgotten corner of Glamorgan, which may account for its rich community life with its blacksmith, baker and village shop. Few tradesmen called from outside the village, but one exception at the beginning of the century was Jones the Flannel who visited once a month in a horse-drawn van carrying rolls of Welsh flannel.

Sadly many of the lovely old cottages have disappeared all along the coastal roads which hold so many memories for me. Many of them have been replaced with holiday chalets and retirement bungalows for people from Cardiff and England who have also taken over the old restored cottages in other parts of the Principality. Things are easier now but there was a time when the holiday homes of the English were being bombed or set on fire in the distorted cause of nationalism. It used to make me so angry: the Welsh after all are happy enough to hear the tinkle of English money in their tills. Ironically, it is the Welsh language which was supposed to give the Welsh back their national pride and identity that has in the event proved to be an instrument of conflict.

(overleaf) *Ebb tide . . . once you could have walked right across Cardiff Docks from boat to boat as they waited to take iron and coal from Wales to the far corners of the world. Now they lie empty.*

125

The Welsh Language Society was formed in 1962 as a result of a speech by Saunders Lewis, then in his sixties, who talked on BBC radio about the possibility of the Welsh language dying out. This sparked off a wave of Welsh nationalism with some younger people refusing to register their babies, unless the necessary documentation was bilingual. The society's intention was to persuade local authorities to make the language a requirement in planning applications, which some saw as a subtle way of keeping the non-Welsh-speaking English out of new village homes. The society maintains that it does not want Wales to become isolated and wants a common policy of Welsh education, particularly in the Anglicized areas. They are helped in their work by a substantial government grant although they say this is insufficient. They claim the formation of the Welsh language TV channel and the revival of Welsh arts and traditions as their successes. The nationalists were given their biggest boost, however, by the hasty Welsh Language Act passed in 1967. The Act dealt with the use of Welsh in legal proceedings and on forms and documents.

In 1961 26 per cent of the population spoke Welsh, and although the figure had fallen to 19 per cent in 1981, the decline has been halted, helped by the fact that Welsh is now widely used in primary school.

My mother married two Welsh speakers and I do still regret that I was not taught to speak Welsh as a child. I took lessons from a Welsh minister from Clydach Vale as a teenager because to be a pupil teacher you needed elementary Welsh. It was a very simple test: the Director of Education himself used to ask in Welsh what your name was and where you lived. You couldn't really fail.

But some of the more modern emphasis seems foolish to me. It is only in recent years, for example, that it has been decided that the Welsh name for Cardiff, which has served us well down through the ages, is Caerdydd, a word I had never seen before, although it is possible that it did once appear on an ancient map.

As Secretary of State for Wales I inherited a Welsh Language Committee which had been set up by my predecessor Cledwyn Hughes. It was their task to translate the difficult words from English to Welsh and they went to great pains to find a Welsh word where clearly one had never existed before. Like 'taxi', for example, which is now written at all our railway stations as 'tacsi'. The arguments are endless and the results often banal, even

(above) *Slowing down . . . the steel works at Port Talbot which we all thought was going to bring prosperity to the area but gradually the work-force has been slimmed down to less than half the original 12,000.*

(right) *The empty sea . . . from this entrance into Cardiff Docks the merchantmen of the past would sail into the Bristol Channel, leaving the estuaries of the Taff and Ely, and skirting Penarth Head and church.*

(overleaf) *Stormy weather . . . the autumn clouds hover above Bardsey Island as the wind whips up the sea lapping the Lleyn Peninsula.*

in place names. So you see the experts, as usual, don't agree and the results we see on forms and signposts are a strange compromise between BBC English and Welsh Office Welsh. The irony is that the new names would probably not be understood by the great Welsh princes.

I certainly do not want to see the language die but it must be wrong that, when senior appointments in Wales are being discussed, the decision often comes down to whether or not the applicant can speak Welsh. Can that be right? Opportunities for jobs and promotions, particularly in government or institutions like the BBC, ITV, the Post Office or the Police, are far better for those who are bilingual. And that is a great weapon in the hands of the Welsh Language Society because parents quite naturally believe their children should learn Welsh in order to get the best jobs. But that is dreadfully unfair to large parts of the country where English is the language and where Welsh has never been spoken.

Nothing escapes now, not even the motorways, where you will see the sign 'Diwedd' which means the end of a diversion. A friend of mine who is a great student of Welsh tells me that it is rather strong language for a road sign as it really does mean the end, the grave, the final solution. Traffic signs did in fact cause me great concern as Secretary of State. After a great battle it was agreed that we would have road signs in both languages. But inevitably the fight moved into the next stage: which language was to be on top, English or Welsh?

I took the view that on motorways, particularly where people were going past at speed, they would look at the name on the top and if they did not recognize it at once their eyes would be off the road for longer as they searched for a familiar name. So English won on grounds of safety! It was only a temporary victory for commonsense as many signs were defaced. English does still appear first, but on a much smaller scale as many local authorities conceded and gave the extremists what they wanted. Nor were the nationalists even-handed: in some parts of Carmarthenshire I found public pathway signs marked 'Llwybr troed'. Here were people telling me all the time about being bilingual and yet they would not use English to let people know where they could have a walk. It seems extraordinary but there are people who see even the supplementary use of English as a threat to the Welsh language.

I well recall when the Welsh Language Society was being led by

a man called Dafydd – David – Iwan, a very popular folk singer. He led a group who asked to come and see me in the Welsh Office when the civil servants were opposed to my meeting them. It was a Saturday morning, and they were put in the conference room to wait for me. As Secretary of State you get accustomed to people standing up when you enter a room. They remained seated. I said: 'Don't bother to stand up', and went to my seat where I greeted them in Welsh before immediately saying that if they wanted a proper understanding of their point of view, they should speak to me in English. We managed very well, though achieving very little, but I don't think they ever realized that my main concern was that they would never leave the room and we would end up with a sit-in at the Welsh Office.

I would guess that only about half-a-dozen people in the road where I live in Cardiff – and it is a very long road – will actually speak Welsh to any decent standard. Cardiff is not very strongly Welsh speaking, but neither is the Rhondda nor Merthyr. Yet aren't these the most Welsh places of all? Many think of the Rhondda as being Wales, because it is Welsh in temperament: it's emotional, loves music, loves drama and has all the Welsh characteristics.

But much of the Welsh language is very beautiful. Tonypandy, for example, means the sound of the watermill and one of my very earliest memories in Tonypandy is of seeing an enormous wooden wheel on the side of the old mill near Pandy square alongside the stream that babbled its way down from the mountain. My mother was born in that house and it therefore had a very special significance for me. It is a pity that the idea of conservation was not as widespread sixty years ago as it is now; when the wheel needed renewing because the wood was rotten it was just removed. I often think that our Welsh names are very much like those of the Indians in America. The name gives a description of the place; the next village north of Tonypandy in Rhondda is called Llwynypia, Magpie bush; there is Pentre which means village; Treherbert – tre, as for the Cornish, means town so that is Herbert's town.

Nevertheless, the argument that it is the language that makes a nation is simply not true. It is not the language that decides your loyalty to a country. If it was, the Scots, Americans and Canadians would be in a bad way! The other irony in the Welsh Language Society's insistence that all official forms and documents should

Princely castle . . . Caernarfon Castle where the Princes of Wales are presented to the people. It was here that I first came to know Lord Snowdon in his role as Constable of the castle when, with the Duke of Norfolk, we planned the investiture of Prince Charles as Prince of Wales in 1969.

be bilingual was that the Welsh could not afford the enormous cost on their own and depended heavily on a massive subsidy from the English. Nobody realized, I am sure, just how much going bilingual would cost.

The Welsh Office, which was formed by Harold Wilson when he won the 1964 General Election, was dominated by the Welsh language issue but faced a series of crises in its early years, when if the truth were told it was really looking for things to do. By definition, it was a nationalistic department. When the Welsh Office was set up, application forms for jobs were sent around all government departments inviting Welsh people in particular to move to the new department in Cardiff. They all knew it would be a rapidly developing establishment with chances of fast promotion so they came from all over Whitehall.

The greatest crisis any of us ever had to deal with was the Aberfan disaster of October 1966 which transcended politics and national frontiers. Grief and guilt does indeed cross boundaries. At the time I was Minister of State for Wales and I swore that however well reasoned or well intentioned the advice, I would never take the slightest risk with people's lives. After Aberfan all of us in the Welsh Office were highly sensitive about trouble in the mining communities. Everybody was blaming the Coal Board for negligence, not just because they had tipped waste coal over a stream on the mountainside, causing a great build-up of water which suddenly came crashing down on innocent people, but rather because nobody had believed that such a disaster was possible.

The horror of Aberfan, never far from my mind at that time, came vividly back to me on 23 December 1968 when I arrived in Cardiff from London on the evening train to be met by a Deputy Secretary at the Welsh Office who told me that there had been a 'little trouble' at Maerdy in the Rhondda Fach. Apparently a horseman riding near the dam had fallen down a hole and it seemed that the ground was giving way. Naturally, he said, everything was under control and there was no need for me to go up. The memory of Aberfan was too close and I decided to go up to the Maerdy Dam on the Lluest-wen reservoir and a meeting was called for 10.30 pm of all the local officials including the police and fire chiefs.

Ted Rowlands, MP for Merthyr Tydfil, was my Parliamentary Secretary and he came with me to the meeting in the schoolroom packed full with officials who told me that they had already consulted a civil engineering firm in London. They had said that there was no immediate danger to the communities. It was getting towards midnight by now but I said I wanted to have that advice confirmed before I went home to sleep. It was quite a drama. I telephoned the civil engineer in London with the Chief Constable standing at my side to listen to the conversation as I said, 'I'm told that you have said there is no danger to the people of Maerdy and that I need not evacuate.' He agreed that was right.

'Well now, one moment,' I said. 'I want you to speak up because the Chief Constable is standing at my side listening to this conversation. I want to be absolutely sure after Aberfan that I am not placing the community in danger. Are you saying there is no danger?' There was no doubt in his voice as he said 'Yes.'

So we went back into the room to meet all the officials and I said I had had a conversation with the engineer who had assured me that there was no danger. Just as I was speaking I received a message to say that I was wanted on the telephone. It was the engineer who, like me, had decided to play safe. He said: 'Secretary of State, I have been giving further thought to what you asked me and I cannot guarantee that there is no danger.'

The meeting had gone on for a long time with everybody being given the opportunity to state their view, so that when this telephone call came it was nearly 4 o'clock in the morning. We turned people out of their homes at 4 o'clock after I had told them that I had now been advised that the civil engineer could not guarantee their safety. Until they were safe, I told them, I was not prepared to go to my bed in Cardiff. The engineer had also told me that if the dam did break, there could be up to 12,000 casualties as the water would pour down into Pontypridd eight miles away. I decided to evacuate the area then and there.

The area was evacuated to the schools which were already lit up and staffed as the local authorities had thought I might order the evacuation. I went around myself with the workers knocking on doors to get the people – old and young – to come out. The lights were on in every house as people stood in readiness, having seen the television news reporting the danger in Maerdy. They were afraid to go to bed and they were right to be afraid because if that dam had gone, even the people in the top roads would all have been drowned. If the dam had broken it would have been one of the biggest disasters in our history. You just don't gamble with the safety of people.

(overleaf) *The tranquillity of Wales . . . this valley on the road from Pontsticill to Cefn used to shake to the trains that once used the now abandoned rail viaduct from which the photograph was taken. Where the trains once thundered, now weekend climbers come to practise their techniques for use in the mountains.*

The evacuation made big news and a press conference was held the next day when one councillor protested that it was wrong to inconvenience people. There was only one reply: it was better to inconvenience them for one night than have them end up in a cemetery. In any case I had been at Aberfan and I was not prepared to gamble with the people's lives if there was the slightest chance of a disaster. I would have been failing in my duty if I had not taken the precautions. What interested me at the time was that no one else was prepared to take that responsibility – neither the chief officers of the local authority nor the police. They all kept saying: 'It's your responsibility, Secretary of State.' One official did give me advice: 'Don't do it – you'll be ruined.' I thought then and I believe it now: better me ruined than a community dead.

The emergency which had begun on 23 December did not go away. By 12 January 1969 engineers, firemen and voluntary labour were fighting against time and rain to pump out hundreds of tons of water from the reservoir at the top of the valley. Engineers were worried about the condition of the 70 year-old dam and some 2000 people had left their homes, including 130 elderly and infirm people along a 6 mile stretch of the Rhondda Fach Valley. The 5 foot by 6 foot hole above the water level had caused no undue alarm until crumbled clay began to emerge from a pipe causing fears that the clay core of the dam was eroding. The 20 acre Lluest-wen reservoir, fed by five mountain streams, is 3 miles above Maerdy and holds 242 million gallons. The risk area included the villages of Maerdy, Ferndale, Wattstown, Ynyshir, Tylorstown, Porth, and Trehafod.

More than 1300 children attending seven valley schools were taken to higher ground. Five hundred miners due to begin work at Maerdy pit were sent home. The weather was so terrible that a RAF helicopter was called in to ferry men and materials. Fifty volunteer miners built sandbag dams to block feeder streams; nearly a hundred engineers worked on the operation, five pumps and twenty-eight siphons taking water out at about a million gallons an hour. Letters were sent from Rhondda Council to 2048 homes advising householders that if they received a warning they were to move to ten schools and two halls on higher ground. The twelve day emergency ended on 25 January after a conditional safety certificate was issued by the engineer in charge and everybody was allowed to return to their homes.

We were very lucky it was not worse – the dam could have

broken while we were there in the meeting and we could all have been washed away. Some people still believe that I made the decision too quickly. But on the Sunday after it was all over, the Church in Wales at Maerdy held a thanksgiving service heralded by the bells pealing out in gratitude that a community had been saved – I know now that a real danger had been avoided.

The Welsh Office, at that time working from old buildings in Cathays Park, Cardiff, began to be given new powers. At last we were being given things to do! On the very day that I was given responsibility for health in Wales, the Government published a very damning report on Ely Hospital, Cardiff. Ely Hospital had six hundred beds and three senior doctors for subnormal and severely subnormal patients. The 1969 report revealed that the patients were knocked about; that there were indescribably filthy conditions in the children's ward; staff were pilfering food, and nursing standards in male wards were, to say the least, old fashioned.

A committee of inquiry of three people headed by Sir Geoffrey Howe had been set up by Richard Crossman, Secretary of State at the Department of Health and Social Security. I knew I was going to take over the hospitals in Wales when I heard Crossman's press conference on Ely. I was a fool to allow him to introduce it. He was an intellectual bully and made the most of the report, laying all the blame on the nurses. What a great fighter he was sitting in his room at the House of Commons.

The next day I went down to Ely to meet the hospital staff, and of course they were furious. They had had a terrible press and were prepared to be angry with anybody. We were all on our guard, not least because the TV cameras had been let in and I particularly remember one red-headed man in the front row who immediately attacked me: 'You're the MP for this constituency, why have we never seen you before?' It was the most damaging thing that an MP could be told and I had to plead guilty as I had only been once before. The whole thing was on the TV news that night with the red-headed man being very angry that the nurses had been accused of stealing from the patients. About six weeks later I was in my office in Cardiff and a note was brought in and pushed before me saying the police had raided the home of the red-headed nurse and found it full of things belonging to the patients. I wrote one word across the top: 'Prosecute'.

I was determined that the Welsh Office should do all it could to improve Ely Hospital, and we did. Among our problems, however, was that of a doctor found guilty by the inquiry of signing death certificates without going in to see that the patient was dead. I took a very serious view of the doctor signing a death certificate without satisfying himself of the cause of death, but I was told that he had taken the word of nurses.

Again I was reminded of experiences in my own circle of near friends. A friend of my mother's in the Rhondda valley was in her coffin and the night before her funeral was seen by another relative to have blinked. She was not dead at all. When I told my medical adviser this, he agreed that it was a very interesting story but clearly he did not believe me. I told him that the lady concerned was still living in Upper Gunner Street, Ynyshir, Rhondda. The doctor then agreed that my anxiety was justified.

Whenever I look at a map of Wales and see the names of towns and villages I am usually reminded of some incident or people that were particularly connected with them. The Vale of Glamorgan and its coast, for example, while beautiful in themselves, are forever imprinted on my mind because of my mother and her long struggle to walk again. Inland and atop a high hill is Abertillery and the old Six Bells mine which, like so many of the pits, suffered a terrible explosion. To get to Abertillery you have to drive up a terrible winding hill which I remember one of its MPs, Cliff Williams, described as having so many bends it was like a snake in a temper. When I preached in one of the local Methodist churches I remember saying that the journey to Abertillery was like the journey to Paradise: it was long and hazardous but very worthwhile when you arrived.

Another of Abertillery's MPs was George Daggar, a highly gifted economist but embittered because Clem Atlee would not give him a job. Daggar had the most sarcastic tongue of any man I have ever met, although we got on well enough. During the period I went missing in Greece in the early fifties (the story is told fully in my memoirs), he looked after my constituents. I shall never forget his greeting when I returned: 'Thank God you're back. I had to preach your bloody sermons.' And that from a militant non-believer! Whatever anybody does to the Welsh they will never blunt our sense of humour.

CHAPTER SEVEN

OF HOPES
AND
MEMORIES

Mary Tudor is reputed to have declared: 'When I am dead and opened, you shall find "Calais" lying in my heart.' Edward I must surely have felt like that about Wales. It consumed both his treasury and his army. The impressive fortresses that he began nearly eight centuries ago still have an intimidating air as they stand as silent sentinels right across Wales. One of the ironies of time is that these ancient castles have survived long enough to serve Wales as a magnet, drawing tourists from around the world when they were firstly intended to keep the Welsh in. It was during my time as Secretary of State for Wales that control and management of the castles was transferred from the former Ministry of Works to the Welsh Office.

In post-war Wales massive unemployment caused by decline in all the basic industries indicated the inevitability of revolutionary change in attitudes to work. The past century has witnessed the rise and fall of industrial South Wales: we have reached the end of an era. It is now vital for leaders in industry and in politics to strive to find new values to maintain parliamentary democracy in the coming era. As we hover on the threshold of the computer age, when less and less manpower will be required on our factory floors or behind office desks, plans for a shorter working life and for education in the constructive use of leisure are imperative.

As we enter a time when much greater wealth will be created by far far fewer people, we will survive as a democracy only if we provide a fair society. This means a just division both of opportunities for work and of sharing in the wealth created. There is no evidence that major rethinking along these lines is under way, but time is running out. Tomorrow's world will only be worth living in if changes essential to a just society are planned for while we still have time. The Wales of tomorrow will need more than history and scenery to guarantee its sons and daughters the quality of life to which they are entitled.

My years from childhood into youth were hard, but there was always the chance of a better life for ourselves and for those dependent upon us. The great escape route was education, yet now that alone is not enough. We all know of highly educated, highly motivated young people who cannot find work. Frustration and desperation can so easily set in, made worse by the expectations that a modern society has come to assume as a right.

The demands in Tonypandy in the 1930s, where expectations were low, were basic. Life centred around the chapels, the pubs,

A lost generation . . . a single memorial to a nine-year-old boy brings back the memories of that terrible day in Aberfan on 21 October 1966 when 116 children and 28 adults perished.

Aberfan 1986 . . . a deserted street at nine in the morning with just a dog and a child in the town that has never really recovered.

the pits, the cinema and the fast-growing working men's clubs. With the sense of humour typical of South Wales, the clubs were all given their special names. There was the Monkey Club – I never did know why – and the Greasy Waistcoat which was supposed to be named after the kind of people that used it, but the Conservatives had the best clubs in the valley, although there were very few Conservatives.

Dad Tom, my stepfather, was considered to be the best billiard and snooker player in the Rhondda and was a member of Llwynypia Conservative Club simply because it had the best billiard table in the valley. I remember how cross he was when the Tories insisted that those who belonged to the Conservative Club should actually vote Conservative. So he had to leave, even though there were good relations between the Labour supporters and the Tories, perhaps because there were so few of them and we knew they didn't stand a dog's chance of ever getting elected.

Now Tonypandy has changed. I always go back for the Mayor making and when I went in May 1985 I was appalled to see the state of the old Central Hall, founded by my grandfather and his generation which had meant so much to all of us. When I saw how it had been vandalized – all the windows had been broken – I felt ashamed as my memories of active worship and real service to the community came flooding back. I told the council that I would prefer to see it erased. Three months later the ground had been cleared and building of a shopping centre had begun. The buildings of the Tonypandy I knew so well will soon be no more but the community still has that fierce pride that I remember so clearly.

Amongst my memories are the summers during the Depression when the Rev R.J. Barker, a crusading middle-class Englishman who was then the Minister at the Central Hall, started chapel holidays in Ludlow, mostly paid for by outsiders. Now, as president of a fund for the aged which raises money to give holidays to people who could not otherwise have one, I can't help remembering that at one period I had a holiday at a reduced price thanks to others. The holidays from the Central Hall were really more like camps. We all used to pile into an open lorry with our rucksacks and tents and had a marvellous time. I suppose we would all have been in our late teens or early twenties.

There was not much money about then and I still don't know how my mother managed to take us three boys when we were very small to Swansea once a year for a week at a boarding house. We used to take all the food so that Mam had only to pay for the overnight room. There are two particular memories that I have, one of the fun we used to have on the railway there. Those trips were very exciting and there used to be a great deal of shouting. It was a steam train with open top carriages like a tram car and would run right around the bay from Swansea out to the Gower Peninsula.

My other memory of our Swansea holidays is less happy. One Sunday the three of us had been down to the beach and stopped to look at a clock that had been made of flowers. A man in a dark suit came up to us – I realize now that he was a preacher – and asked me if I had been to church that day. I told him that we hadn't and by way of explanation added: 'We're on holiday.' He was an arrogant man: 'Tell your parents from me that they should be ashamed of themselves bringing you up this way.' He of course did not know that we did not have a father and that we were being brought up by just our mother. When we told Mam, she explained to us that naturally we would not have gone to a chapel or a Sunday school where we did not know anybody. I realize now that she would probably have felt embarrassed for strangers to see that she was on her own without a husband. There was a stigma attached to one-parent families in those days: she even stayed away from our own chapel for a long time because she could not face the congregation.

I had no idea talking to that man on a little bridge in Swansea looking down on a clock made of flowers that the time would come when, as Secretary of State, I would advise Prince Charles to make Swansea, the birthplace of Dylan Thomas, a city when he went there at the end of investiture week. I had a terrible battle because officials in England protested loudly, strongly and bitterly that I should not agree to Swansea being a city because there were bigger places in England that had not been so honoured. I replied that England was England and Wales had to have its own measurements. I was always very fond of Swansea and the countryside around because of my boyhood holidays. Once you leave Swansea you are in an agricultural country where the sheer beauty of the scenery is matched by the coastline all the way up from Pembrokeshire along Cardigan Bay to Harlech Castle, looking down on Cardigan Bay up to the Lleyn Peninsula, which on the map looks like an elephant's trunk poking down.

I keep my memories fresh by staying in touch with the people

(above) *Victoriana One . . . weren't Victorian engineers wonderful! This ornate mini-castle is no more than the control tower of the outflow at Pontsticill Reservoir and dates back to the 1890s.*

(right) *Victoriana Two . . . this magnificent railway viaduct, built without any modern machinery and now abandoned, ran from Pontsticill to Cefn, near Merthyr Tydfil.*

(overleaf) *Away from it all . . . Castle upon Alun, typical of the rural tranquillity that has always existed in Wales alongside the toil and sweat of the old industries. Here the families of the miners and the iron workers found their peace.*

and visiting the places as often as I can, but it is Tonypandy that has pride of place for me. There are still many living there who I remember as neighbours and friends. The first telegram I received when I took the title of Tonypandy was from the Mayor of Rhondda. The Council organized a concert to celebrate my title and invited two valley choirs with very special reputations, the Pendyrus and the Treorchy Male Voice Choir. They had never sung together before but out of kindness to me they came to a black-tie concert. There were about two thousand people in the sports centre in the middle of the valley and the two choirs sang together with the conductors changing over so that Treorchy conductor conducted the Pendyrus and the Pendyrus conductor conducted Treorchy. There were children from my old school and people from the Methodist church; everything that had touched my life was represented in those celebrations.

My Wales is already becoming a memory. Physically, the landmarks are disappearing; spiritually, there has been a parallel demolition, only a tiny proportion of the community there now having anything to do with either church or chapel. So the Rhondda that I grew up in has vanished, but the Wales of my grandfather is returning.

I look up at the hills that were bare all through my boyhood because the trees had been cut down for pit props and for use during two world wars. The Forestry Commission has been at work and the green valley is again being bordered with a tree-studded hillside. The beauty that my grandfather knew appears to be coming back. The grime of the coal industry, the smoke that used to come from our very high chimney stacks no longer pollutes the air. But as the old works go, the people there need new industries, as coal was new to my grandfather's generation.

If work can be found, the Rhondda of tomorrow will have the vitality, the charm, the beauty and the warmth of the Rhondda my grandfather knew when he went there in 1872. When, as he used to tell me, a squirrel could swing from tree to tree from one end of the valley to the other.

I hope too that the people will always keep the right to wander over the hillsides. My happiest memories are linked with the walks along the tops where there is no sign of human life. Right up there you cannot see the bottom of the valley, all you can see is the glory of nature. Those walks must be preserved for future generations to enjoy as we did. If I know anything of the spirit of the Rhondda, they will be.

RIP . . . *the grass and weeds provide a blanket for the burial places of generations of the Welsh, who have seen hardship and prosperity, and whose sons and daughters now face new challenges.*

Memories . . . sorrow and memory are universal; here a family lie in peace tended by a relative in the land where family ties and influences remain an essential part of life.

Whenever I go home to the Rhondda and see the changes that have taken place, the disused pits and boarded shops, I am reminded of the fact that the people of the valleys have always had to fight to survive. Many of them now, as their parents and grandparents did before them, are fighting to save the communities which have endured so many disasters, both economic and natural. There will be doubters, but I for one believe the unchanging spirit of the Rhondda will live on.

INDEX